Helion & Company Limited
Unit 8 Amherst Business Centre
Budbrooke Road
Warwick
CV34 5WE
England
Tel. 01926 499 619
Email: info@helion.co.uk
Website: www.helion.co.uk
Twitter: @helionbooks
Visit our blog http://blog.helion.co.uk/

Designed and typeset by Farr out Publications, Wokingham, Berkshire
Cover design by Paul Hewitt, Battlefield Design (www.battlefield-design.co.uk)

ISBN 978-1-804510-19-3

British Library Cataloguing-in-Publication Data
A catalogue record for this book is available from the British Library

We always welcome receiving book proposals from prospective authors.

CONTENTS

Acknowledgements 2
Acronyms 2
Introduction: The Wider Picture 2

1 Spread Thinly Across the Globe 3
2 Malayan Emergency 13
3 Politics in the Region post-1957 27
4 Brunei Revolt, 1962–1963 34

Bibliography 48
Notes 49
About the Author 54

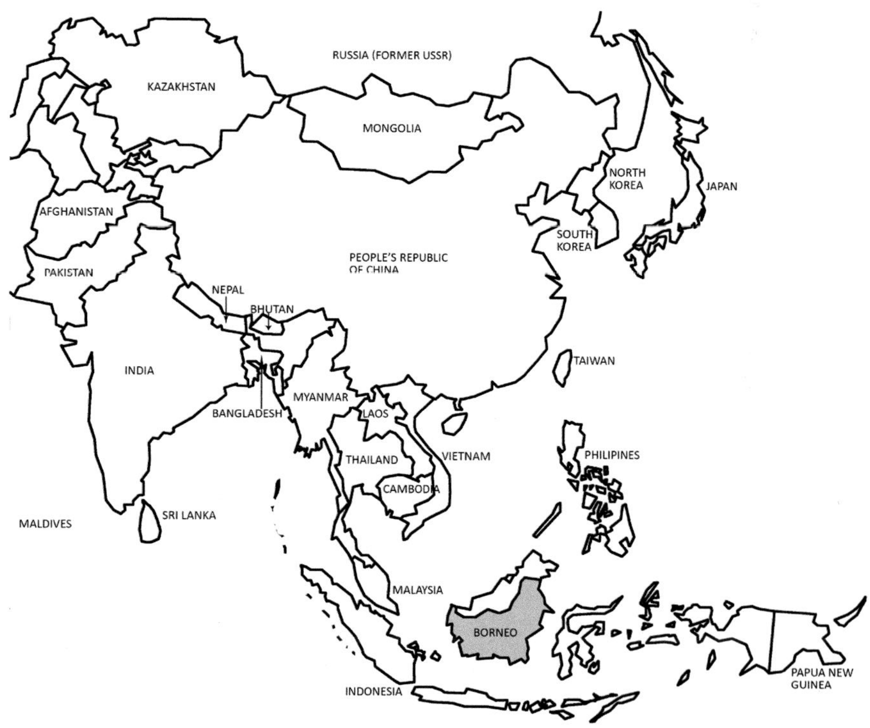

Note: In order to simplify the use of this book, all names, locations and geographic designations are as provided in *The Times World Atlas*, or other traditionally accepted major sources of reference, as of the time of described events.

ACKNOWLEDGEMENTS

Many thanks to Professor Ian Beckett, who has gone through the manuscript correcting where required and commenting when needed. Also, to my wife Estelle who was busy writing her own book but managed to keep me on track, and my father S. Davis who was stationed in Penang during the Confrontation serving with the 2nd Battalion Royal Green Jackets. Thank you one and all. Finally, to Series Editors Tom Cooper, Bill Norton, and to Albert Grandolini: Tom and Bill who have had to answer questions of the most obscure nature and managed to find the answers while Albert has sourced the photos that have been used in both volumes. Any other mistakes are mine and mine alone.

ACRONYMS

AMDA	Anglo-Malayan Defence Agreement
GOC	General Officer Commanding
HQ	Head Quarters
MCP	Communist Party of Malaya
MRLA	Malayan Races Liberation Army
NATO	North Atlantic Treaty Organization
PKI	*Partai Komunis Indonesia* (Indonesian Communist Party)
QOH	Queen's Own Highlanders
RAAF	Royal Australian Air force
RAF	Royal Air Force
RNZAF	Royal New Zealand Air Force
SEATO	South East Asia Treaty Organization
TNKU	*Tentera Nasional Kalimantan Utara* (National Army North Kalimantan)
UN	United Nations

INTRODUCTION: THE WIDER PICTURE

The Confrontation, or *Konfrontasi*, remains a neglected area of modern military history although the closure of the official documents by the successive reductions of the 50 Year Rule (1958), 30 Year Rule (1967) and 20 Year Rule (2010) have now enabled historians the chance to study the military and political thinking that prevailed during the 1960s. At its heart was a stand-off between Indonesia under the leadership of Sukarno and Tunku Abdul Rahman's Malaya/Malaysia after 1963.

Sukarno was a charismatic leader and believed that Indonesia should be at the forefront of Asian expansion, viewing Tunku Abdul Rahman as a puppet of the British government. It was Sukarno's actions against the formation of Malaysia comprising North Borneo, (Sabah), Brunei, Sarawak and Singapore, that laid the ground for what was to become known as the Confrontation. At times it was a very intense conflict with cross-border incursions undertaken into the Indonesian side of Borneo coupled with a strong pinch of plausible denial. Indonesian forces also carried out similar operations.

Britain was supported by Australia and New Zealand after initial reluctance due in part to the fear of upsetting Sukarno and viewing it as a purely British problem. Commonwealth forces, along with Gurkha companies and British regiments, were deployed to halt Indonesian incursions using the same principles of fighting a jungle-based war and using the lessons learnt during the Malayan Emergency and, in some cases, improving on the then current thinking. What also has to be taken into consideration is that British forces were in the late 1950s and 1960s spread very thinly across the globe. On the ending of the Second World War, Britain's initial action was to downsize the regular army, which meant that regiments had to deploy smaller forces which were supplemented by National Service personnel; these postings were also alongside

Premier of Malaya/Malaysia Tunku Abdul Rahman. (Albert Grandolini collection)

President Kennedy and Sukarno on Sukarno's visit to the US. (Albert Grandolini collection)

Britain's NATO obligations. So, when military outbreaks occurred in Aden, Cyprus, Dhofar, India, Kenya, Korea, Palestine and Malaya, to name a few, it stretched the British army nearly to breaking point.[1] Moreover, Britain's smaller army still had commitments within South East Asia: the formation of the South East Asia Treaty Organization (SEATO) in 1954 committed regiments to tours of the area, primarily stationed at Changi Base in Singapore and Penang. The formation of SEATO came at a time when British and Malayan forces were already involved in supressing the forces of the Malayan Communist Party.

This book will therefore start by looking at other conflicts with British involvement and then the Malayan Emergency and how it shaped British military thinking in fighting a jungle-based counter-insurgency operation. It will then turn to Brunei and the subsequent revolt, which was the perceived catalyst for the Confrontation. This study will not be purely military based for the historian must look at the bigger picture the politics of those involved. There were behind the scenes machinations by the USA, Russia, China and the United Nations (UN) in aiding, abetting or holding to account those involved. Readers who require further reading should refer to the bibliography at the end of the book.

Table 1 shows the leaders from the Second World War and later whose leadership also covered the Malayan Emergency and the Confrontation.

Table 1: Veteran Political Leaders of the Malayan Emergency and the Confrontation

Leader	Dates	Party
US Presidents		
Harry S. Truman	1950	Democrat
Dwight D. Eisenhower	1953	Republican
John F. Kennedy	1961–1963	Democrat (assassinated)
Lyndon B. Johnson	1963	Democrat
Malaya/Malaysia		
Tunku Abdul Rahman	1957–1970	UMNO (United Malay National Organisation)
Indonesia		
Sukarno	1945–1967	Indonesian National Party
Britain		
Clement Attlee	1945–1951	Labour
Winston Churchill	1951–1955	Conservative
Antony Eden	1955–1957	Conservative
Harold Macmillan	1957–1963	Conservative
Alec Douglas-Home	1963–1964	Conservative
Harold Wilson	1964–1970	Labour

1
SPREAD THINLY ACROSS THE GLOBE

Palestine

During the First World War Britain issued a statement which would become known as the Balfour Declaration, named after its author Arthur Balfour the then Foreign Secretary. Its intent was to support the establishment of a national home for the Jewish people within Palestine which, at the time, was part of the Ottoman Empire. The thinking behind a Jewish homeland had started when war was declared against the Ottoman Empire in 1914. The Declaration was in itself quite controversial with its aims and ambiguity. Indeed, the opening words showed support for Zionism – a first for a major power – while the wording of a "national home" was vague, having no precedent in international law of the time. The boundaries of this new Jewish homeland were also not specified; the British government confirmed that the borders of this new homeland within Palestine did not cover the whole of Palestine.[1] The wording of the document was to create further problems later on, leading to an escalation of violence which the British seemed hamstrung to contain.

General Sir Willian Jackson used the quote that Britain built her empire in a fit of absent-mindedness: Britain's acceptance of the League of Nations' Mandate to establish a Jewish home in Palestine turned out to be a high-minded error of judgement.[2] The League of Nations was the forerunner to the United Nations (UN). Established on 10 January 1920 arising from the agreements and mandates reached at the Paris Peace Conference, the League continued until on 20 April 1946 ceasing in its current form, but many aspects were used in the creation of the UN.

In 1920 the League of Nations had entrusted Britain with the Mandate for Palestine. The British Army, aided by the local Arab populace, succeeded in expelling the Turks from Palestine. For their part the League endorsed what had been outlined in the Balfour Declaration to create a home for the Jews. The Arab population at the time was 600,000 compared to the 55,000 Jewish population living within the country. The Arabs were bemused at this and alluded to this fact stating that the League and notably Britain had got their priorities confused.[3] The steadily rising numbers of Jews flowing into the country forced the Arabs to openly revolt in 1936. By 1939 the revolt had been quelled but it had taken 17 British battalions to achieve this. Although the Arabs had been defeated militarily,

An Otter light reconnaissance car patrolling in Palestine. This Canadian designed vehicle saw service with a number of Commonwealth nations and the RAF Regiment during the Second World War and later saw service with the Jordanian and Syrian militaries. It was typically armed with a light machine gun in the turret – in this example a Bren gun – and a Boys Anti-tank Rifle or a second machine gun could be fired through the smaller of the two hatches on the left side of the front hull. (Albert Grandolini collection)

they had succeeded in forcing the British to the negotiation table, signing a white paper in March 1939 restricting Jewish immigration to 75,000 for the next five years, with no more immigrants without prior agreement from the Arabs. The Jews now felt aggrieved by this turn of events.[4]

The outbreak of the Second World War put more strain on the Arab-Jewish relationship within Palestine. The Arabs politically blundered when the Grand Mufti of Jerusalem sided with Hitler, thus alienating any British goodwill and assistance. Many Jews aligned themselves with the British although this also created problems as a number of Jews saw this as a way to 'bend' the rules around entry into Palestine. As the Arabs had capped entry into the country, in order to gain entry into Palestine Jews could serve in the Middle East halting German expansion through joining the British Army, or gain support within the United States from the large number of Jews residing there, who had money and political influence, in order to get the cap lifted.[5] Churchill was all for arming the Jewish populace and using them to fight the Germans, but in reality only one brigade was raised and that was posted to Italy; the Chiefs of Staff considered the risk of alienating Arab opinion too great.[6]

However, not all Jews were pro-British. One such faction was the Stern Gang or *Leham Herut Israel* (Hebrew Freedom Fighters) led by Abraham Stern, who had arrived from Poland in 1940. Stern's views were so extreme that the group broke away from the Irgun which at the time was viewed as an extreme of the Jewish paramilitary groups within Palestine. Stern sought to side with Hitler to drive out the British thus allowing European Jews to migrate to Palestine, while allowing Germany to govern the country.[7] To this end the Stern Gang launched a series of guerrilla attacks against the police and Army. Initially, Stern was successful in attacking military and civil forces, but by February 1942 Stern's luck ran out while engaged in a firefight with the police: he was shot dead along with other members of the gang. This defeat of the Stern Gang did not mean the end of anti-British feeling within Palestine, or indeed of the Stern Gang. Later in the year a former follower of Stern, Menachem Begin, took up the leadership mantle, becoming leader of the Irgun in 1943, and by 1944 launched a revolt against British rule. Begin and the Irgun, however, did not attack British military forces as long as they were fighting the Germans. Despite this, police stations were still attacked, with many causalities as a result. Begin, like Stern, cut ties with the more moderate Haganah; a people's army which had been sanctioned by the British Administration.[8]

This cycle of violence was to continue with the Irgun targeting tax offices, CID branches and immigration offices. British and Jewish public opinion was equally shocked by these attacks that caused a wave of anti-Zionist feeling.[9] Indeed, the Jewish Agency condemned the Irgun and the Hagana took steps to hunt down Irgun sympathisers. Against this backdrop Churchill and Roosevelt were moving ahead in their support of the Zionist cause against the advice of their foreign policy advisors. However, events were to later change their support, especially that of Churchill, whose close friend Lord Moyne, British Minister in Cairo, was assassinated by the Stern Gang. This led Churchill to become less inclined to support the Zionist cause, moving to a more neutral position with a slight tilt towards Arab interests and flying in the face of American pressure coming from the White House.[10]

In October 1945, the British security forces in Palestine were a mixture of Arab, Jewish and British personnel. The Palestine police comprised 5,000 British, Arab and Jewish constables under British officers. Along with the Arab-manned Transjordan Frontier Force and the Bedouin Arab Legion, British military forces consisted of 1st Division, which was resting and retraining after the Italian campaign, while 6th Airborne Division was also in the process of being posted there as part of the Middle East Strategic Reserve. Both of these could be used to aid the police if required. Reinforcements, if required, could come from the Independent 7th Infantry Brigade stationed near Jerusalem under GHQ command, while naval and RAF forces were also stationed in the eastern Mediterranean.[11]

Perhaps emboldened by Irgun's successes, many Jews rose up in open revolt against British policy. 31 October 1945 saw the destruction of the Palestine railway network which was crippled in 154 places, along with trains and locomotives being disabled. This was followed up by the sinking of police patrol craft along with some damage to the oil refinery at Haifa. Although these attacks were not intended to cause any loss of life, one policeman and two railway workers were killed.[12] These hit and run attacks continued for the

Refugees and British soldiers on a dockside during the Palestine troubles. This is one of a series of photographs, this particular one showing British troops on the wings of the ship's bridge removing banners identifying the vessel in English and Hebrew as the Hagana Ship *Unafraid*. Most of the troops wear the distinctive "Helmet Steel Airborne Troops" and camouflaged Denison smocks, identifying them as being from 6th Airborne Division. The soldiers are armed with Lee Enfield .303 rifles, and with the exception of one or two with canvas bandoliers for ammunition, have little additional equipment or webbing. (Albert Grandolini collection)

remainder of 1945. 1946 continued as 1945 had finished, with a series of attacks on three RAF airfields along with continued disruption of the railway lines. On occasion, Irgun's luck ran out, with one attack on the railway resulting in Irgun being ambushed by 8th Battalion of the Parachute Regiment: Irgun took heavy losses and the survivors were forced to surrender. In retaliation, Irgun counterattacked, murdering seven members of the Parachute Regiment who were relaxing on the Tel Aviv waterfront.[13]

The escalation of violence continued with the bombing of the King David Hotel on 22 July 1946. This attack came about after the British after had searched and screened Jewish homes and arrested those whose sympathies lay with Irgun. Operation Agatha, as it was termed, was a success with 600 weapons captured.[14] The significance of the King David Hotel was that it housed government and military personnel, and although heavily guarded it was still a hotel open to the public and was supplied by outside contractors. This allowed Irgun to infiltrate the hotel, delivering milk churns filled with explosives to the ground floor café. Irgun was also meant to have telephoned a warning to the hotel, but this was mishandled with the warning coming too late to evacuate personnel. In fact, in the act of planting the explosives the terrorists were surprised and a gun fight ensued. The resulting explosion within the hotel caused the deaths of 91 military, government and civilians, and also caused one wing of the hotel to collapse.[15]

In the aftermath of the bombing, Tel Aviv was cordoned off and the city was subsequently searched. This involved 17,000 troops who were successful in recovering arms and arresting sympathisers, although again Begin manged to evade capture. The increase of violence within Palestine meant more troops were required to police the cities and key areas. By July 1946, a year after the cessation of hostilities of the Second World War, 27,000 troops were in the country.[16] Even Ernest Bevan, now Britain's Foreign Secretary, was at a loss to solve the Palestine problem, referring the matter to the UN. The UN decided that the partition of Palestine would be the best course of action, and this was announced in November 1947. Irgun now took the fight to the Arabs and the British, and this was to continue into 1948. Irgun changed tact unsuccessfully to take on the British Army in a conventional war, rather than the hit and run tactics which had been previously proved to work, and they were beaten on numerous occasions. They were outmatched by British forces and suffered many casualties. By May 1948, Sir Alan Cunningham, the High Commissioner, left Palestine on HMS *Euryalus* with the Government of Palestine transferring to the United Nations Commissioner; it had been 30 years and five months since the army under General Allenby had first entered Jerusalem by the Jaffa Gate.[17] The Army had received a bloody nose on many occasions and found itself in a no-win situation, often being blamed by both sides, but the regiments posted there had acquitted themselves well. Total losses had been 20 British officers and 203 soldiers killed. This would not be the last time that military forces would see action in this area but Korea was about to erupt, bringing its own set of problems.

The Korean War

Two years after the withdrawal from Palestine, British forces were once again stretched across the globe when in June 1950 the Korean War broke out. Although the Korean War was relatively short, only lasting three years, its legacy still casts a shadow over the area to this day. From a British viewpoint, Korea was not high on its list of priorities, being primarily concerned with the regeneration of Malaya and Singapore. Britain viewed Korea as an American problem in halting Soviet encroachment into the area. However, what alarmed British strategists was the prospect of fighting communist powers on two fronts separated by 11,000 miles of sea.[18] After the Second World War, Korea was recovering, having being used by the Japanese as the main food provider for the Imperial Army.[19] Shortly after the Potsdam Conference held on 6 August 1945, the Russian 25th Army under Colonel General Ivan Chistyakov invaded Korea occupying the northern provinces as far as Pyongyang. It had been agreed that US forces would disarm the Japanese south of the 38th parallel, and the Nationalist Chinese would disarm them north of this line. This quick entry into Korea by the Soviets caught the Americans completely off guard with no available troops near enough to counter; the nearest were in Okinawa but were being used in mopping-up operations.[20] While America and Russia argued about who should withdraw, an impasse continued along the 38th parallel. It was not until 25 June 1950 that the North Korean Army, consisting of 89,000 men in seven divisions and three independent units, entered South Korea in six closely packed columns, achieving

An RB-29 Boeing Superfortress camera platform of 31st Reconnaissance Squadron over Korea in 1951. While offering excellent range and enough space to carry mission-related equipment, the type proved much too slow and thus vulnerable to interception by the latest Soviet MiG-15 fighter jets. (Bill Norton collection)

A row of North American F-86A Sabres at an air base in (South) Korea, in June 1951. Already busy with the build-up of conventional forces for a possible showdown with the USSR, even the USA were short of the latest combat aircraft for deployment to the Korean War. Another limiting factor was the low number of suitable air bases. (Bill Norton collection)

total strategic surprise. Facing them were the Republic of Korea's forces, which were woefully understrength, with four divisions and one regiment totalling 38,000 personnel. Of this figure, some had been held in reserve, and many were on furlough. The military hardware available to the South was also not up to the standards of North Korea. North Korea had T34 tanks, which the South could not counter as they had no anti-tank armament. The Americans had deemed it unnecessary to supply tanks to the South, arguing that the road infrastructure was inadequate to cope with them.[21]

The United Nations had to respond quickly to the invasion, in part because the Soviet Union was boycotting the Security Council. British and Commonwealth troops began to arrive to support American and South Korean forces already in country. Lieutenant General Sir Horace Robertson from Australia was given overall command of the British Commonwealth Occupation Forces consisting of Australian, New Zealand and British troops, with Britain once more sending the majority of military personnel. Subsequently this force became known as British Commonwealth Forces Korea (BCFK) although still under Australian command.

The fighting element of BCFK was the 1st Commonwealth Division, which consisted of four infantry brigades supported by armour, artillery, combat support and combat service support units: 25 Canadian Infantry Brigade, 27 British Commonwealth Brigade, 28 Commonwealth Infantry Brigade and 29 Independent Infantry Brigade. The Canadian and Independent brigades were wholly Canadian and British formations, while 27 and 28 Brigades were Commonwealth entities. In their entirety, BCFK contained units from Australia, Canada, India, New Zealand, South Africa, and Britain.[22] Further stretching Britain's military forces, Korea could also be viewed as a National Serviceman's war, as the majority of the personnel were not regular army.[23]

Casualty figures show that many countries were not immune to personnel being killed or injured. Casualty figures for the British, Commonwealth and American forces are shown below:

516 Canadians killed
1,100 British killed, 2,600 injured
37,000 Americans killed, 92,000 injured
339 Australians killed, 1,216 injured
42 New Zealanders killed
110,000 Chinese killed 380,000 injured

2–3 million civilian deaths
990,968 South Korean deaths
1,550,000 North Korean deaths[24]

Again, this put further pressure on stretched British forces posted globally. The Korean War has never technically ceased as it concluded with an armistice. Thus, an uneasy peace sits on the demilitarized zone between North and South Korea.

Kenya

While the Malayan Emergency was unfolding in Asia, Britain faced a similar problem in Kenya when members of the Kikuyu tribe rose up over the misappropriation of land dating back to 1915, and growing resentment of how the European community had prospered on this land after the Second World War. It culminated in 1952 with a state of emergency which lasted four years. The Kikuyu launched hit and run attacks on settlers and settlements. In what would become known as the Mau Mau Rebellion, the Kikuyu involved in this guerrilla style war did not discriminate between European settlers and African farmers. Africans comprised the majority of the victims, with most fatalities amongst men, women and children alike caused by dismemberment using pangas (machetes), while livestock were disembowelled or hamstrung.[25]

Avro Lincoln bombers of the RAF on an apron in Kenya. Although obsolete and slow, the type was heavily armed and possessed excellent range, which is why it was deployed in numerous 'small' conflicts around the globe in the 1950s, including the Kenyan emergency. (Albert Grandolini collection)

In September and October 1952, a number of Africans loyal to the government were murdered; numerous reports of oathing and intimidation were received, and on European farms cattle were maimed and buildings burned down.[26] The newly installed Governor, Sir Evelyn Baring, had no choice but to declare a state of emergency three weeks after arriving in Kenya, asking for military aid to protect the country.[27] The first regiment to arrive in Kenya was the 1st Battalion Lancashire Fusiliers, flown in from Egypt. Even with this regiment in country it did not stop attacks on villages. On 22 March 1953, in what would become known as the Lari massacre, 74 men, women and children were killed. This was then followed up by an attack on a police station in Naivasha, killing two policemen, releasing 150 prisoners, and absconding with a large arms cache. On paper it seemed that the combined military and police forces were unable to stem the violence within the country. A further call for reinforcements was sent to Britain, which saw the arrival of General Sir George Erskine who was appointed C-in-C (Commander-in-Chief). Erskine now commanded 39 Brigade, made up of at various times of two to three battalions of British troops, and 70 Brigade comprising five or six battalions of King's African Rifles. There was also the Kenyan Regiment, mostly made up of Europeans, the East African Armoured Car Squadron, and a battery of East African Artillery along with two RAF squadrons: one of Harvards and the other of Lincolns.[28]

Checking identity papers in Nairobi. The British soldier on the left carries a Bren light machine gun, while those in the centre and on the right carry the No.5 Mk I 'Jungle Carbine' version of the Lee Enfield rifle. All have '44 Pattern webbing and wear a distinctive fusilier 'hackle' on their berets. Note that the soldier in the centre of the picture has a bayonet fixed to his rifle. (Albert Grandolini collection)

Baring had delayed too long with the introduction of a state of emergency: it was a case of catching up then jumping ahead of the Mau Mau. The Mau Mau's political leaders were rounded up and arrested, including notably Jomo Kenyatta who would eventually become the country's president.[29] However, this did not slow down the rate of attacks on civilian farms and livestock. Recruitment into

Patrolling in the Kenyan environs. The British radio operator carries a No.4 rifle, whilst his companions are armed with spears. It appears that there is also a bow carried by another man largely obscured by the radio operator. (Albert Grandolini collection)

The patrol of three de Havilland DHC-1 Chipmunk training aircraft of the RAF seen on patrol over Kenya. (Albert Grandolini collection)

the Mau Mau ranks was one of an oathing ceremony to instil loyalty within the recruits. The naivety of the recruits was played upon as many believed that if they broke the oath they would suffer as a result.[30] To counter the continuing rise in violence, British forces adopted unorthodox tactics which proved to be very successful. Under the leadership of Frank Kitson and Eric Holyoak they created what was to become known as counter gangs or pseudo-gangs, which would infiltrate Mau Mau cells and in most cases successfully capturing them.[31] This was the way forward for the rest of the campaign and by 1956 the insurgent uprising had run its course.

An African soldier guarding Kikuyu prisoners. Note the small "spike" bayonet affixed to the rifle and the large machete worn on the belt. (Albert Grandolini collection)

Cyprus

To the modern traveller Cyprus seems like an ideal holiday destination. The population of Cyprus is a mixture of Greek-speaking Cypriots and a larger Turkish population.[32] During the 1950s it was a hotbed of terrorist attacks against British forces stationed there. These attacks were organised by EOKA (*Ethniki Organosis Kyprion*), which had the support of the Greek civilian population, and its agenda was for greater ties with mainland

Stop and search patrols in a mountain village in Cyprus. (Albert Grandolini collection)

A Ferret MK 2/3 and Land Rovers on patrol in Cyprus in 1964. The Mk 2/3 Ferret was manufactured with heavier side and rear armour compared to earlier variants and had a Browning .30 machine gun in a one-man turret. The insignia on the front turret is that of The Royal Dragoons (1st Dragoons). (Albert Grandolini collection)

Greece.[33] The eventual fighting also had religious overtones as Archbishop Makarios also wanted stronger ties with Greece. In 1954, the 2nd Battalion the Green Howards and 2nd Battalion Royal Inniskilling Fusiliers arrived in Cyprus from Egypt in part to aid in the relocation of Middle East HQ. These regiments were soon used in anger as serious rioting erupted in Nicosia and Limassol resulting in two civilian fatalities after military forces opened fire. Against this background a retired Greek Army colonel and self-styled general, George Grivas, began to form guerrilla cells within the mountains to fight back against British forces.[34] It was not until April 1955 that the intensity of the fighting increased.

The British response was to appoint Field Marshal Sir John Harding whose remit was to take the fight to EOKA. By November 1955 a state of emergency had been declared. British forces were greatly increased with the Royal Horse Guards and 1st Battalion the King's Own Yorkshire Light Infantry joining the fight alongside the Parachute Regiment, Royal Marine Commandos and the Gordon Highlanders.[35] In comparison, EOKA's military wing amounted to 350 personnel but was supported by a passive wing which was quite successful in intimidating the local population into submission.[36] Harding adopted the command and intelligence structure that had been used successfully in Malaya with troop strength increased to 20,000 personnel. Harding hoped to strike a decisive blow but was hampered by troops being relocated to Suez in 1956 and Jordan in 1958. Unable to mount a successful counter-insurgency in the mountains aside from 'Operation Pepperpot,' which was semi-successful in clearing EOKA from the Troodos, Harding changed tact and targeted towns with curfews successfully locking down any outside aid to EOKA. By December 1958 EOKA announced a ceasefire. The final death toll amounted to 90 insurgents, 104 British servicemen, 50 Policemen, and 238 civilians. There was, however, sporadic fighting between Greek and Turkish forces that continued into the 1970s.[37] British forces policed the Green Line from 1964 for the UN and following the Turkish invasion of 1974.[38]

The Suez Crisis

Perhaps the most significant incident after the Second World War was the Suez Crisis. The British government had hoped it would be a case of business as usual within the Middle East as it had been when returning to South East Asia. At the start of the 1950s it was deemed important to retain the large military base in Suez as well as the air bases located in Iraq, this was also in part to stem the Soviet influence that was encroaching into the area.[39] Britain still had treaties with both Iraq and Egypt but had failed to renegotiate the Anglo-Egyptian treaty of 1936 which would have preserved the British use of the Suez base in case of need while conciliating Egyptian nationalism through the withdrawal of Britain's obtrusive military presence.[40] Instead, the British relied on treaty rights and the manpower stationed at the base numbering in the region of 80,000 men.[41] It could be argued that the British had stuck their heads in the sand hoping to avoid any conflicts; this however, was not to be the case. The rise of the Muslim Brotherhood from the late 1940s resulted in the most powerful mass organisation in the Middle East. Coupled with

Nasser signing the arms deal with Czechoslovakia. (Albert Grandolini collection)

the problems in Palestine and the subsequent victory of Israel over Egyptian and Arab armies in 1948, this was the last nail in the coffin of British influence in the area.[42] If Britain was to do something it needed to act now.

In the aftermath of the humiliating defeat at the hands of the Israelis, the Egyptians now viewed the British as betrayers over the way that Palestine had been handled. For their part the British stayed put.[43] This entrenchment led to an escalation in violence against British personnel, coupled with the local labour force downing tools and refusing to work. For their part the British lost patience, and in an effort to disarm the auxiliary police attacked a barracks where they were stationed, killing 41 Egyptians. This was answered with attacks on British-held property, resulting in a further loss of life with 11 British killed. It was also the death knell for the Egyptian monarchy: in June 1952 a military coup under the leadership of Neguib and Nasser overthrew the monarchy allowing the army to assume control of the country.[44]

For the British it seemed like an ideal opportunity to try and broker a deal with the new regime. Talks were opened and by 1954 an agreement was reached between Nasser and Eden, allowing the withdrawal of troops over a 20 year period, but the base could be used if an external threat developed to any Arab state in the Middle East, or Turkey (which was a NATO member).[45] The new use of the base in Suez has similarities to what Britain would have to agree to in Singapore in the 1960s. However, there were some misgivings. Churchill tried to block the agreement as it entrusted the Suez Canal to Nasser, but, staying put would highlight the division and worsening relations with Egypt, and show Britain in a bad light with other parties in the Islamic world, as well as tying down 80,000 personnel and exposing them to potential attacks.[46]

Nasser on the other hand had different ideas and was astute enough to think that the concessions he had gained showed that the British were in a weak bargaining position. The pressure that Nasser was experiencing at home and abroad meant that Egypt and Britain were on a collision course. Indeed, Nasser's leadership was tenuous at best, having survived an assassination attempt a day after the signing of the Suez agreement. Nasser blamed the Muslim Brotherhood which allowed him to subsequently ban the organisation and hang its leaders.[47] Nasser, and his views on Egypt, were very similar to what Sukarno in Indonesia hoped to achieve within South East Asia: that his regime and Egypt's independence were not safe until it was the main Arab power within the Middle East with Cairo as its centre.[48] Nasser's paranoia came to a head in 1955 with the signing of the Baghdad Pact between Iraq, Turkey and Britain, coupled with close British ties with Jordan as the final straw, culminating in the Suez Crisis 18 months later.[49] Nasser in a masterclass of political savviness played on widespread beliefs that any Western defence pacts were thinly veiled attempts at colonialism in all but name, while also playing on Arab disunity, especially against Israel, which was due in Nasser's view to British interference. Nasser also sought and obtained the help of Saudi Arabia whose royal family were the historical enemy of its Iraqi and Jordanian counterparts. This gave Nasser the ear of Washington as Saudi Arabia had close ties with the US.[50] The Egyptian Army had historically obtained its arms from Western suppliers. In a surprise move Nasser obtained a new deal with Czechoslovakia to supply modern weaponry.[51]

If it was not enough that Britain was losing face in the Middle East, Britain had also lost US support. Due in part to Britain siding with Iraq, Washington in an apparent volte-face withdrew its support for the Aswan dam which had been the main incentive to keep Nasser in line. Nasser's next move was swift and devastating: 26 July 1956 saw the nationalisation of the Suez Canal, having left a long enough gap that the withdrawal of British military forces meant that a swift response was impossible.[52] Washington was not going to aid Britain with its plans to retake the Canal: it was an election

The superior flight performance of the MiG-15 came as a big surprise for the US and allied airmen over Korea. Unsurprisingly, the Americans were delighted when one of the North Korean pilots defected with his jet to the South, in 1953. His jet is seen here – wearing US markings – while undergoing testing at Okinawa in Japan, later the same year. (Bill Norton collection)

A Grumman F9F-2B Panther from the (reservist) squadron VF-721, embarked aboard the USS Boxer (CV-21) seen in a shallow dive while making a strafing pass with its 20mm guns, over Korea, on 15 July 1951. (Bill Norton collection)

year and any show of force was strongly opposed. Eden, boxed into a corner with only France seemingly willing to help, came up with a plan to allow Israel to suddenly attack Egypt, thus allowing British and French forces to intervene to defuse the situation. October 1956 saw Israel attack Egypt, followed up a week later by British and French forces landing at Port Said and under the pretence of halting the opposing forces started to wrest control of the Canal back from the Egyptians. Washington however, had other ideas and threatened Eden with restrictions and pressure, firstly on sterling, and then by holding back American oil at a time when the supply of Middle East oil was low.[53] By December both Britain and France had withdrawn their forces and Britain's humiliation was now complete within the Middle East. Further embarrassment was to follow when Jordan ripped up its treaty with Britain. Iraq, an ally of Britain, saw its leaders overthrown and subsequently murdered. With British dominance in the area broken it could in theory pave the way for Soviet expansion, while Israel stopped being a local issue and was thrust onto the world scene. It was US intervention that dealt the death knell for Britain in the Middle East and with it any chance of resecuring the Suez Canal and overthrowing Nasser.[54]

Rows of Piasecki H-21 or 'Flying Bananas' on board an American aircraft carrier (serving as aircraft transport) en route to Vietnam. The US engagement in that country was indicative of how American military influence was spread around the globe. (Albert Grandolini collection)

American Perspective

Traditionally, America has to some degree adopted what can be termed as splendid isolation, making no attempts to empire build and, in many respects looking inward rather than globally. This can be seen in both world wars: entering reluctantly in the First World War while Pearl Harbor forced its hand in the Second World War. After the war however, America became enmeshed in the politics of South East Asia and in some cases stopping any communist threats within the area. Vietnam and Korea being the two keynote wars, America was in some countries happy to supply arms, aircraft and tanks while in others putting pressure on former colonial rulers to give up their ties to the area.

With subsequent US presidents Truman, Eisenhower and Kennedy, there was a differing of politics, policies and aid within South East Asia. During the Truman administration it was seen that the Dutch insistence on holding onto their colonies was doing more harm than good. In order to get the Dutch to give up their claims on the East Indies, the US applied pressure by threatening to withdraw Marshall Aid that was being allocated to the rebuilding of the Netherlands. The Dutch reluctantly accepted American terms and withdrew from South East Asia but were semi-appeased by the American moderator insisting that the Indonesian government would shoulder the external debt of the old East Indies. But much to the annoyance of Sukarno, they allowed the Dutch to retain the western portion of New Guinea (West Irian), which led to successful Indonesian pressure to oust them.[55] This empowered Sukarno to try and stop the formation of Malaysia in 1963.

A Piasecki H-21 being used to relocate farmers of South Vietnam into so-called 'strategic villages', in order to isolate – but also to protect – them from the Viet Cong insurgency. (Albert Grandolini collection)

The US influence in South East Asia could be interpreted as an arms dealer with a smidge of economic bolstering. The French were recipients of both arms and economic aid while trying to control the Viet Minh insurgency in the mid-1950s. During Truman's presidency, Britain had enjoyed a good working relationship; this was to change when Eisenhower came to power. British policy makers

A Piasecki H-21 helicopter seen conducting casualty evacuation operations, early during the US involvement in South Vietnam. (Albert Grandolini collection)

The aftermath of a railway derailment caused by Viet Cong insurgents in South Vietnam. (Albert Grandolini collection)

and government distanced themselves from Eisenhower's seemingly heavy-handed approach to solving global problems. Washington seemingly wanted to use the policy of massive retaliation in order to quell a local conflict, which may or may not have induced Peking or Moscow to play an active role. This was highlighted in 1954, when military action at Dien Bien Phu provided the French with a very bloody nose. The Eisenhower administration wanted to provide a strong show of force against North Vietnam. However, the softly, softly approach adopted by Britain at the Geneva Conference flew in the face of what Washington wanted to do, creating resentment in Washington in what was seen by many there as appeasement to a communist backed regime.[56]

Moving forward to the Malayan Emergency and the Confrontation, US involvement was one of peace broker and arms supplier, as well as provider of aid loans, especially in the case of Indonesia. Although Britain, with perhaps the Suez Crisis embarrassment still fresh, viewed America as perhaps more of a hindrance than a help. America, however, had its own problems within South East Asia, namely Vietnam, which was taking up a lot of American manpower, munitions and politics. The Vietnam War would come to overshadow the Confrontation and continue after the latter had ended. The Vietnam War caused long term problems within America with mass protests, draft dodging and anti-war movements during the 1960s and early 1970s. America would view the Confrontation as purely a British problem that could be solved with minimal interference from America.

2 MALAYAN EMERGENCY

After the Second World War, South East Asia did not enter a period of post-war peace. From 1945 there were a series of wars: of these the longest one fought was Vietnam with the cessation of hostilities in 1975. The summary below shows just how violent the area was post-Second World War:

1945–1949: Indonesian-Dutch Campaigns
1945–1954: I Indochina War (French in Indochina)
1946–1955: Hukbalahap Insurrection in the Philippines
1948–1960: Malayan Emergency
1950–1953: Korean War
1955–1975: II Indochina War (USA in Indochina)
1963–1966: Borneo Confrontation
1963–1975: War in Laos
1967–1975: Cambodian Civil War

There were periods of semi-peace but these were short-lived. Of the above the Emergency and Confrontation will be discussed in-depth, while the remaining wars will be looked at to provide an overall picture of what was going on during the post-war period. The Indonesian-Dutch campaign was a means for Indonesia to oust the Dutch, successfully waging a war of words and violence against the Dutch and gaining independence in 1949.[1] Simultaneously, in the Philippines, the Hukbalahap Insurrection began. A group indoctrinated with communist ideals nearly succeeded in overthrowing the government and gaining a foothold in the region.[2] Following on from this was the Korean War, which, as already related, was a far more serious affair involving many countries, with the US being one of the major players.[3] Although relatively short-lived, the loss of life was very severe for the civilian population and military forces on both sides.[4] After a two year period of what looked like peace, although the Emergency was still being fought, the Vietnam War erupted onto the world stage and until its conclusion in 1975 would dominate world news being in many respects the first televised war.[5] Cambodia in 1967 saw a small-scale communist uprising against the government of Prince Norodom Sihanouk. Sihanouk quite successfully held back the communist forces led by Pol Pot, while trying to maintain Cambodia's neutrality, although North Vietnamese forces were using the country as a staging point for incursions into South Vietnam along the Ho Chi Minh Trail. However, Sihanouk was overthrown by his prime minister, subsequently forming a government in exile. Cambodia went through a period of chaos with many atrocities against the population while the opposing armies fought to gain overall control of the country.[6] Laos was another former French colony which suffered a period of warfare which resulting in a communist victory.[7] This allowed the Confrontation to be fought without the eyes of the world looking at it.

In 1948, Malaya having survived the privations of the war in South East Asia was slowly rebuilding its infrastructure and economy and its standing within the world. British officials also returned to the area to continue its colonial policy after being forced to abandon Malaya during the Second World War by trying to maintain the façade of business as normal. Malaya and Britain however came to realise that the previous working relationship would no longer work in post-war Asia. Soon after British troops returned to the peninsula, Whitehall announced a new political arrangement known as the Union of Malaya.[8] This was an attempt to juggle the ethnic groups of Malays, Chinese and Indians by improving the political situation of the Chinese and Indian population. It failed to gain ground as it was opposed by the Sultans and Malayan Civil Service. However, in December 1946, Whitehall began laying the groundwork of what would become the Federation of Malaya, although the plan was not officially ratified until 1948.[9]

Emergence of Communism as a Force

It was against this background of bumbling bureaucracy that the Communist Party of Malaya (MCP) emerged from the aftermath of the war in a strong position under leader Lai Tek.[10] The MCP at least on paper had disbanded its field army and turned in its arms. However, the MCP had in reality buried arms caches in the jungle and retained a cadre organisation in the form of the Old Comrades Association.[11] Lai Tek was astute enough to realise that he and the MCP were not strong enough to seize control outright. Tek has been described as a charismatic leader who worked his way up to the post of Secretary General of the MCP Central Committee through his own initiative and with the help of Special Branch.[12] It later transpired that Tek was a triple agent who had worked for the

South Vietnamese (ARVN) soldiers armed with US-supplied M1 Garand rifles and M1 carbines move through a burning village. (Albert Grandolini collection)

Japanese, British and the Communist Party.[13] Anybody who posed a threat to Tek's push to the top was removed at night, in some cases by the Special Branch.

However, by 1947, the party had begun to suspect that Tek was not as loyal as he appeared, with repeated accusations made by members, and police raids on key party held buildings after Tek had visited. Tek, seeing that the writing was on the wall, absconded with party funds and went into hiding, leaving Singapore some months later.[14] This betrayal led to a power struggle between the inexperienced leadership and the more radical members of the party. The lack of good quality leaders in the senior and middle level ranks led to much uncertainty and was to plague the party for years.[15] Chin Peng, who replaced Tek as Secretary General, becoming its de facto leader was to remain in the role for the duration of the Emergency.

The Move Towards Violence

In 1947, violence within the country was at an all-time high. This was highlighted by the government's inability to maintain law and order, coupled with a police force which had practically disintegrated at the end of the war, along with the loss and destruction of its network of informers and records.[16] The police force was in the throes of being rebuilt but this took time which in 1947 the government did not have. Examples of the violence included 40 Chinese bandits raiding the village of Klian Intan, shooting a customs officer and Chinese villager, and then proceeding to pillage the village. Another involved an arms cache being discovered outside of Kuala Lumpur, with a haul consisting of 10,000 rounds of ammunition and 30 assorted weapons. In retaliation for the arms cache being discovered the night train from Kuala Lumpur to Penang was derailed, while a lorry load of policemen was ambushed with considerable loss of life.[17] All these attacks were in part carried out by Chinese under the banner of the MCP.

The opening acts of violence against Europeans occurred in June 1948 in the small town of Sungei Sipat, situated north of Ipoh in the state of Perak. Rubber plantations operated by Arthur Walker, John Allison and Ian Christian were attacked by Chinese operatives and, they were murdered in their offices or while on their rounds.[18] Another plantation manager, Donald Wise, escaped with his life when his jeep broke down; three Chinese would-be assailants who had arrived at Wise's office grew suspicious at the delay and left the plantation.[19] Rubber plantations were not the only European sites that were targeted. Tin mines were also attacked in an attempt to cripple Malaya's export infrastructure. As the news of these attacks filtered out, they came to the attention of the Chinese Affairs Office and it fell to Robert (Bob) Thompson to investigate what had occurred on these sites.[20] Chin Peng in later life denied that these murders were on the order of the Central Committee, apportioning the blame as result of overt enthusiasm for revenge at the local level coupled with a serious lack of command and control at the state level.[21] Thompson upon arriving at Elphil took stock of what was before him, but was unable to do anything until reinforcements arrived in the form of a company of Gurkhas, which was subdivided and allocated to guard the other estates that had not been attacked.[22] Thompson then proceeded to the estate of Sungei Sipat, spending the night there in case it was attacked again, and the following day returned to Ipoh.[23]

Further atrocities were carried out: a Chinese headman was strung up for refusing to pay a subscription to the MCP. His attackers hacked off his arms while his wife and daughter were forced to watch. In Ipoh, a meeting of planters was convened where they aired their frustrations at the lack of government protection.

MCP Leader Chin Peng in a photo taken at the Bailing Talks. (Albert Grandolini collection)

The High Commissioner, Sir Edward Gent, dismissed the planters' protests as 'alarmist.'[24] Gent, during his tenure, was an unpopular High Commissioner. It was not until a face-to-face meeting with planters that Gent relented and imposed a state of emergency on the areas which had been attacked. *The Straits Times* went as far as printing the headlines 'Govern or get out.'[25] Gent then extended the emergency to the whole of Malaya and, the following month to Singapore.[26]

Prior to issuing the emergency orders, Gent had been using what have been termed banishment orders. These proved useful in deporting Chinese and non-British subjects. Anthony Short has shown that it had been an effective weapon in dealing with gangs, extortionists and criminal intimidation.[27] However, it had its flaws, British Indians had immunity from the orders and subsequently became prominent in disturbances and acts of violence.[28] The MCP realised that if they stayed within towns or villages, at some point they would either be arrested by government forces or the army.

As their next move it was logical for the MCP to use the jungle as it allowed them a safe base of operations to conduct attacks on forces and extort supplies from villages and towns before slipping back into the jungle and evade any acts of reprisal from British or government forces. For British and Malay forces it was a case of having to relearn the art of fighting in the jungle, while the MCP had not the need to do so, and with their arms caches and camps they had the upper hand for the foreseeable future. The MCP once it had relocated to the jungle formed the Malayan Races Liberation Army (MRLA) as the armed front of the MCP.[29]

British Response

A week after Gent had issued the emergency orders he was recalled back to London, but while waiting to land in Britain his plane was involved in a mid-air collision killing all on board.[30] With Gent's death it now created a power vacuum which was not filled for three months until the appointment of the new High Commissioner Sir Henry Gurney. Until Gurney had been brought up to speed and was in the country it fell to Malcolm MacDonald, the Commissioner General for South East Asia, to try and get the campaign against the MCP underway. However, Macdonald had no real power within the Federation and could only cajole and prod those in power to act on the escalation of violence.[31] From a military perspective the newly arrived General Officer Commanding Malaya (GOC), Major General C.H. Boucher, inherited the anti-bandit campaign. It could be argued that Boucher was wearing two hats as the Commissioner of Police, H.B. Langworthy, was ill and near to resigning his post. The rest of the administration was in the hands of acting officials.[32] Boucher also played up his experience of fighting a guerrilla war assuring everyone that the army would have no difficulty dealing with the MCP. It soon became clear however, that neither Boucher nor the officers under his command had any idea how to fight a successful counter-guerrilla campaign.[33] The mind-set of the officers was locked in a conventional war, which would not work in the jungles of Malaya.

Militarily speaking, the forces stationed in Malaya were reasonably strong, although spread out across the country. In country were six Gurkha battalions protecting rubber plantations and tin mines, with another stationed in Singapore. Royal Artillery personnel were also posted to Malaya primarily to train the Gurkhas as gunners. There were three British infantry battalions: two in Singapore and one in Penang.[34] Despite being a strong force on paper, these battalions were hamstrung by the fact that military forces could only be used in conjunction with police actions and as mentioned earlier, the police force was having to re-establish itself. Indeed, the police force had no Special Branch and lacked people who knew what to look for and how to gather information. The police were also unsure whether to term these forces bandits or communist terrorists.[35] A month after the declaration of the Emergency, steps were being taken to take the fight to the MCP. Ferret Force was created with the onus on taking the fight to the MCP.

Ferret Force was a hybrid of professional and amateur personnel. The idea was first put forward by Bob Thompson after Boucher approached him.[36] Many of the civilians had been in Force 136 which had been created to fight the Japanese in the Second World War. Ferret Force was subsequently led by Lieutenant Colonel Walter Walker, who would later play a key role in the Confrontation. It was Walker's intention that Ferret Force would consist of the following: a British volunteer with local knowledge, a British officer, 12 volunteers from either British or Gurkha regiments, the Malay regiment, a detachment of Royal Signals, Dyak trackers and a Chinese liaison officer.[37] It was during a visit by General Sir Neil Ritchie, Commander-in-Chief Far East Land Forces (CinC FELF), that Walker learnt he was being reassigned to run the Jungle Warfare School at Johore Baru to train reinforcements now being sent to Malaya by the British government. This proved to be the death knell for Ferret Force and by the end of the year it had been disbanded.[38]

The Jungle Warfare School

The creation of the Jungle Warfare School would prove pivotal in taking the fight to the MCP. The school would run six-week training courses, and by the time of the Confrontation this was down to a month.[39] The camp was situated on the site of a former mental hospital at Tampoi chosen for its location and easy accessibility to the nearby jungle. The Guards were the first through the doors with battalion and company commanders – it was Walker's intention to train officers and NCOs, and then they could train their battalions. Towards the end of their course, trainees were sent into the jungle where MCP cells were known to be and put into practice what they had learnt. One class found itself face-to-face with three armed terrorists and managed to kill them all.[40] It proved that Walker's thinking and training were bearing fruit. However, those above Walker were of the mind that now the Guards had been trained the crisis would be quickly and effectively brought under control. Walker was not averse to making public complaints and, at a subsequent demonstration Walker clashed with Boucher and Colonel Nicol Grey, Commissioner of Police, over putting troops and police into armoured vehicles. Boucher suggested that it was too 'defensive minded'; Gray agreed and refused to send any more police to the Jungle Warfare School. Walker's views were vindicated when a police party travelling from Kuala Lumpur were attacked; the soft skinned vehicle they were travelling in provided no protection and all the men on board were killed.[41]

Governmental Response

While Walker was retraining the army to fight in the jungle, Gurney had arrived in Malaya. After a few weeks it became obvious that to take the fight to the MCP Gurney needed to split the roles of running the government and fighting a war. Fortunately for Gurney the right man for the job was recommended for the role of Director of Operations, this was Lieutenant General Sir Harold Briggs.[42] General Briggs had been divisional commander in the 14th Army, a retired GOC Burma, and was now living in Cyprus.[43] The role of Director of Operations had an anomalous position of a soldier who was civilian, directing military operations in support of a civil power.[44] Briggs' arrival came at a time when operations and successful campaigns against the MCP were at a low point. Briggs soon realised that to counter the MCP, the political organisational arm known as the Min Yuen and the MRLA needed to be dealt with in one blow, this would become known as the Briggs Plan.[45] The Briggs Plan also had a third aim of winning over the Chinese squatters who had occupied tracts of government land near the borders of the jungle.[46]

The Briggs Plan

The official title was of the Briggs Plan was the 'Federation Plan for the Elimination of the Communist Organisation and Armed Forces in Malaya,' though 'the Briggs Plan' was in all probability easier to remember. It laid out what was needed to effectively combat the Min Yuen and MRLA.[47] Briggs argued that the police would maintain peace after the military had made safe the surrounding area. The police forces were still weak however through lack of recruits and reliable information. Briggs argued that to gain the trust of the civilian population they needed to feel that they were safe, and the

Lieutenant General Harold Rawdon Briggs. (Albert Grandolini collection)

A later scene showing a pair of Ferret Scout Cars of the Queen's Royal Irish Hussars in Borneo. The circular insignia on the turret front indicates that this vehicle belongs to C Squadron of the regiment. A Westland Whirlwind helicopter of the RAF can be seen passing by overhead in the rear. (Albert Grandolini collection)

police needed to instil confidence that they were up to the task.[48] This could only be achieved by recruitment from a more diverse background. Briggs reasoned correctly that the Min Yuen was able to function with impunity within populated areas because the population had lost confidence in the police force to protect them from gangsters, communist extortion and terrorism.[49]

The Army's role was to dominate the jungle, within a five-hour radius of potential MRLA supply dumps, to take control of the tracks and paths leading to and from the jungle, with military headquarters situated within populated areas.[50] The RAF would also be used to drop supplies, conduct aerial reconnaissance, and assist in attacks when information had been corroborated.[51]

Another aspect of Briggs's plan dealt with the civil administration as this also needed to play its role for the plan to succeed. The current makeup of the administration was unsuited to deal with the Emergency. Each state had its own local government which in turn reported to the Federal government. What was common amongst all of these was the British Advisor who previously had little if any power within each state: he could now play a more active part in Emergency matters leaving the business of running local government to those better suited to the task.[52] Before any operations could be carried out a new framework was created and the existing framework was strengthened. Meetings were held every week and information disseminated between departments. Special Branch personnel were bolstered and Chinese Affairs Officers who could also speak Malay were recruited and sent to villages or squatter areas in preparation for what was to come.[53]

Briggs acknowledged a need to get the Chinese population to trust the government and feel that Malaya, not China, was their home.[54] The Chinese rural populace viewed resettlement with mixed feelings: many needed to be forcibly moved while others went willingly. Many Chinese saw resettlement as a way to escape harassment from either the police and army or MRLA, while allowing them a permanent piece of land to farm.[55] These new villages were not perfect and Richard Stubbs has pointed out that model resettlement villages were the exception. What could not be relocated was destroyed, including in some cases livestock. The cost of materials to build new habitations was 'hiked' up as the government had failed to control supplies. One of the main criticisms of these camps was that potable water and sanitation were not up to standard, with dysentery, malaria and enteric fever occurring, coupled with a shortage of trained nurses and doctors to treat those who had caught various diseases.[56]

These new villages were not immune from attacks, since the protection was provided by Malay special constables who were poorly trained and armed, without proper leadership, and unwilling to lay down their lives for Chinese settlers whom they distrusted.[57] Once these villages had been built the military could begin to clear the jungle, pushing MRLA forces further north. By the end of 1950, 117,198 persons had been moved into 140 new villages, most of which were protected by barbed wire and perimeter lights. By 1951 this number had increased to 385,000 into 429 villages. The following year saw 509 new settlements with a population of 461,822. In the space of two years, half a million Chinese squatters had been brought under effective administrative control, cutting off the MCP/MRLA from a major source of income and support.[58] However, events outside of Malaya would firstly alarm the country, but secondly allowed it to profit by supplying rubber and tin.

Korean War

25 June 1950 saw the outbreak of war in Korea a few weeks after the inception of the Briggs Plan. Initially it was perceived that this war would allow communism to gain a stronger foothold within South East Asia and that Malaya and Singapore would be subsumed into the communist machine. The early successes of North Korea alarmed countries in South East Asia; American forces were drafted in aided by British and Commonwealth forces stemming the tide against the communists and China subsequently entered the war. The situation, however, created a golden opportunity for Malaya. The country's two main exportable commodities were rubber and tin, and countries on a war footing needed these. As a result the economy boomed, with the government and business's profiting from the increased prices that rubber and tin now commanded.[59] By February 1951 rubber had risen to $2.20 per pound while tin

increased to £1,300 per long ton, filling Malayan government coffers from the duties collected: enough to fund the resettlement programme and bolster the monies set aside for the Emergency.[60] The Korean War had a detrimental effect on the MCP as Chinese labourers now saw an increase in wages and jobs, and so were less inclined to support the MCP. The plantations and tin mines could now effectively protect their assets. Indeed, Dunlop, one of the major plantation owners, spent four million dollars on armoured cars and highly trained European security personnel.[61] The Korean War proved to be a major asset in the government's campaign against the MCP, gaining much needed funding for its law and order campaign and the resettlement programme.[62]

Commencement of Military Actions

1 June 1950 saw the start of major operations against the MCP/MRLA starting in Johore, Negri Sembilan and southern Pahang. However, initially, the military build-up failed in its aims of breaking communist control within these areas.[63] This was down to a multitude of reasons; public confidence had not improved with the large influx of military personnel now in the areas; and large scale patrolling on minimum information had not brought any action against the MRLA.[64] Attacks increased in areas that had not been secured; while in Johore after incidents initially dropped, they began to increase due in part to a massive resettlement project which was still ongoing, allowing the MRLA to freely attack camps, plantations, mines and forces.[65]

Another factor which damaged public morale and had not been used to its full potential by His Majesty's Government was deportation. Other proposals put forward by the Malayan government had not been acceptable.[66] If both governments had pushed harder to deport Chinese undesirables, this would have had a two-fold effect. Firstly, it would have improved confidence in the government's response to MCP/MRLA actions. Secondly, increasing public confidence would lead to a more reliable source of intelligence which the police and army could act on.[67] Lessons were learnt and going forward the combined forces began to get results putting the MRLA onto the back foot.

Regimental, Police and RAF Strength

At the start of 1948 available forces that could be utilised to fight the MCP/MRLA comprised 9,000 police and 10 infantry battalions. At the height of the Emergency, 67,000 police, 300,000 Home Guard and 23 infantry battalions were involved.

Police

It was the task of the federated police to protect the local population from terrorist attacks and intimidation. As mentioned previously once recruitment issues were solved, personnel available to the police steadily increased. In part many were recruited from British policemen stationed in Palestine.[68] In 1948, 9,000 police were employed; by January 1951 this had increased to 16,814, reaching 24,427 in 1954. Amongst this latter figure was a special police force comprising of 2,915 personnel formed in 1950 to occupy jungle bases and undertake cross-border incursions into Thailand in pursuit of MRLA forces.[69]

A special constabulary was also formed in each state comprising of Malays to guard plantations, mines and other important installations and to enforce food control. Initially, it numbered 10,000 men in August 1948, but by January 1952 it had reached 44,878, reducing to 23,857 by 1955 when the role was changed from static duties to active patrolling. All police units, Regular and Special, were controlled from a central Federal Police Headquarters based in Kuala Lumpur.[70]

A blow to the MCP plans was the formation of the Chinese Home Guard in 1951, used to guard the new villages constructed under the Briggs Plan. Recruitment into the Home Guard topped 30,000 by the end of 1952 and it proved to be a useful deterrent against MCP/MRLA incursions into the new villages. The Chinese Home Guard was created along the same lines as the Kampong Guards formed in 1949, these were Malay recruited and used to guard Malay villages and totalled 47,000 personnel by 1950. In 1951 the civil defence was reorganised and the Chinese Home Guard and Kampong forces were amalgamated into a single Home Guard unit totalling 300,000 personnel.[71]

Military Forces

Alongside the police forces the military was also to play a key role in subjugating MRLA forces. In 1948 ten infantry battalions were stationed in Malaya and Singapore. By 1950 this had increased to 26 battalions, dropping to 21 in 1957. The strength and composition varied to suit the needs of each state but by the end of 1951, all British battalions contained five companies and 1,000 men. At the start of the Emergency in 1948, troop strength was 10,000 men, reaching 30,000 (of whom half were non-operational).[72] This military force was drawn from around the globe: in 1955 there were six British, six Ghurkha, seven Malay, one Fijian, one African and one Australian battalion, along with a New Zealand squadron of the Special Air Service. Supporting these forces during the Emergency were two armoured car regiments each containing up to six squadrons, one or two field batteries, an artillery regiment, two engineer regiments, one commando brigade, three squadrons of the 22nd Special Air Service Regiment and one squadron of the Parachute Regiment.[73]

Control of the army was decentralised along geographical lines. The four Sub-Districts that existed in Malaya and Singapore in 1948 were reorganised into three Districts in 1949:

- South Malaya District: Johore, Negri Sembilan, Malacca and Selangor;
- Malay District: Pahang;
- North Malay District: Perak, Kedah, Perlis, Kelantan, Province Wellesley and Penang.

Brigade Headquarters was normally located at Police HQ in each state capital, while Battalion HQ was also located within Police District HQ, with Company HQs situated at local police stations. This allowed military forces to supplement police forces when required. This was also the system that the MCP/MRLA adopted.[74]

Royal Air Force

The RAF also played an important role in the Emergency, providing air drops to forces in the jungle, and reconnaissance flights over areas where the MRLA were known to operate. It was not however, a pure RAF operation, with RAAF and RNZAF aircraft being used along with local auxiliary and national air forces. In 1948 aircraft available for use in the Emergency consisted of three squadrons of fighters, four of medium-range transports, one of photographic reconnaissance aircraft and one of flying boats. By July 1954 this had increased to two squadrons of medium bombers, three of fighters, three of flying boats, three of medium-range transport planes, three of short-range transport planes and one photographic reconnaissance squadron, which along with other aircraft gave the RAF 166 aircraft. In addition to these, Royal Navy and Royal Malayan Navy air

Table 2: RAF Units and Aircraft of the Confrontation			
Unit	**Aircraft**	**Base**	**Role**
28 Squadron	Spitfire F.Mk 14, FR.Mk 18	Tengah, Sembawang	Ground-attack, Fighter-reconnaissance
60 Squadron	Spitfire FR.Mk 18, Vampire FB.Mk 5/9, Venom FB.Mk 1/4	Tengah, Sembawang, Kuala Lumpur	Fighter, ground-attack
60 Squadron	Meteor NF.Mk 14	Tengah	Night fighter
45 Squadron	Beaufighter F.Mk X, Brigand B.Mk 1, Hornet F.Mk 3/4, Vampire FB.Mk 9, Venom FB.Mk 1, Canberra B.Mk 2	Kuala Lumpur, Tengah, Butterworth	Light bomber, ground-attack
33 Squadron	Tempest F.Mk II, Hornet F.Mk 3/4	Changi, Kuala Lumpur, Tengah, Butterworth	Ground-attack, fighter-reconnaissance
84 Squadron	Beaufighter F.Mk X	Changi, Tengah, Kuala Lumpur	Light bomber
84 Squadron	Brigand B.Mk 1	Tengah, Kuala Lumpur	Light bomber
81 Squadron	Spitfire F.Mk 18 & PR.Mk 19, Mosquito PR.Mk 34, Harvard T.Mk 2B, Anson C.Mk 19, Meteor PR.Mk 10, Pembroke C(PR).Mk 1, Canberra PR.Mk 7	Changi, Tengah, Seletar, Kuala Lumpur	Public Relations
209 Squadron	Sunderland GR.Mk5, Shackleton MR.Mk 1	Seletar, Changi	General, maritime reconnaissance
205 Squadron	Sunderland GR.Mk 5, Shackleton MR.Mk 1	Seletar, Changi	General, maritime reconnaissance
88 Squadron	Sunderland GR.Mk 5	Seletar	General, maritime reconnaissance
656 Squadron	Auster AOP.Mk 5/6/9 & T.Mk 7	Sembawang, Kuala Lumpur, Taiping, Seremban, Kluang, Changi, Temerloh, Benta, Ipoh, Port Dickson	Observation, light liaison
1325 Flight	Dakota C.Mk 4	Seletar	Medium-range transport
48 Squadron	Dakota C.Mk 4, Valetta C.Mk 1, Hastings C.Mk 1/2, Beverley C.Mk 1	Changi, Kuala Lumpur	Medium-range transport
52 Squadron	Dakota C. Mk 4, Valetta C.Mk 1	Changi, Kuala Lumpur	Medium-range transport
110 Squadron	Dakota C.Mk 4, Valetta C.Mk 1	Changi, Kuala Lumpur	Medium-range transport
FECS	Dakota C. Mk 4 Valetta C. Mk 1/2, York C. Mk 1, Hastings C. Mk 1/2, Devon C. Mk 1, Pembroke C. Mk 1, Anson C. Mk 19, Harvard T. Mk 2B, Auster AOP. Mk 6/T.7, Vampire FB. Mk 9, Venom FB. Mk 1, Meteor T. Mk 7	Changi, Kuala Lumper, Butterworth	Communications
HQ FETW	Valetta C. Mk 1	Changi, Kuala Lumpur	Transport, psywar (to 267 Squadron)

Table 2: RAF Units and Aircraft of the Confrontation *(continued)*

1311 Flt	Pioneer CC. Mk 1	Kuala Lumpur	STOL transport (to 267 Squadron)
267 Squadron	Pioneer CC. Mk 1, Pembroke C. Mk 1 Auster AOP. Mk 6/T.7, Harvard T. Mk 2B, Dakota C. Mk 4	Kuala Lumpur	Short-range transport (renumbered 209 Squadron)
209 Squadron	Pioneer CC. Mk 1, Twin Pioneer CC. Mk 1, Pembroke C. Mk 1, Dakota C. Mk 4, Auster AOP. Mk 6/T.7	Kuala Lumpur, Seletar, Bayan, Lepas	Short-range transport
CEF	Dragonfly HC. Mk 2/4	Changi, Kuala Lumpur	Casevac (to 194 Squadron)
194 Squadron	Dragonfly HC.Mk 2/4, Sycamore HR.Mk 14	Sembawang, Kuala Lumpur, Ipoh, Kluang, Benta	Transport, casevac (renumbered 110 Squadron)
155 Squadron	Whirlwind HAR. Mk 2/4	Kuala Lumpur, Kluang, Seletar	Transport (to 194 Squadron)
110 Squadron	Whirlwind HAR. Mk 4, Sycamore HR. Mk 14	Butterworth, Kuala Lumpur	Transport (ex 194 Squadron)

Table 3: Fleet Air Arm Units and Aircraft of the Confrontation

Ship	Units	Aircraft type	Shore base
Triumph	800 NAS, 827 NAS	Seafire FR.Mk 47, Firefly FR.Mk 1	Sembawang
Theseus	807 NAS, 810 NAS	Sea fury FB.Mk 11, Firefly FR.Mk 5	Sembawang
Glory	804 NAS, 812 NAS	Firefly FR.Mk 5, Sea fury FB.Mk 11	Sembawang
Ocean	802 NAS, 825 NAS	Firefly FR.Mk 5, Sea fury FB.Mk 11	Sembawang
Warrior	811 NAS, 825 NAS	Sea Fury FB.Mk 11, Firefly FL.Mk 5	Sembawang
Centaur	801 NAS, 811 NAS	Sea Hawk FGA.Mk 4, Sea Hawk FB.Mk 3	Tengah
Albion	804 NAS, 809 NAS	Sea Venom FAW.Mk 21, Sea Venom FAW.Mk 22	Seletar
Centaur	804 NAS, 810 NAS	Sea Venom FAW.Mk 22, Gannet AS.Mk 4	Seletar

Table 4: Commonwealth and Malayan Units and Aircraft of the Confrontation

Unit	Aircraft	Base	Role
MAAF (Malayan Auxiliary Air Force)			
Malaya/Penang Squadron	DH.82A, Harvard T.Mk 2B, Chipmunk	Butterworth	Light liaison, reconnaissance
Singapore Squadron	DH.82A, Harvard T.Mk 2B, Spitfire F.Mk 24, Chipmunk	Tengah, Seletar	Light liaison, reconnaissance
Kuala Lumpur Squadron	DH.82A, Harvard T.Mk 2B, Chipmunk	Kuala Lumpur	Light Liaison, reconnaissance
RMAF (Royal Malay Air Force)			
1 Squadron	Pioneer, Twin Pioneer, Chipmunk	Kuala Lumpur	Light transport
RAAF			

support provided coverage of the sea surrounding Malaya by intercepting illegal seaborne traffic, while a squadron of naval helicopters were used for troop lift between 1954 and 1956.[75] Table 2 outlines the RAF assests stationed in Malaya from 1948.[76]

Operations against the Min Yuen and MRLA

On the onset of the Emergency the MRLA had more notable successes than the Malayan government and the army, the authorities having underestimated the gravity of the situation in which they found themselves. During the early months of the Emergency the army and police were trying to stabilise civilian morale protecting essential utilities and industrial installations. Once the MRLA realised that they could no longer operate from towns and villages they retreated to the jungle, leaving behind kill squads which continued to harass and intimidate villages and towns. But, more importantly, it forced the army to turn its attention to clearing these combatants out of inhabited areas. Between 1947 and 1948 attacks against civilians numbered 212 per

Table 4: Commonwealth and Malayan Units and Aircraft of the Confrontation (*continued*)			
3 Squadron	Sabre F.Mk 32	Butterworth	Fighter, ground-attack
77 Squadron	Sabre F.Mk 32	Butterworth	Fighter, ground-attack
1 Squadron	Lincoln B.Mk 30	Tengah	Medium bomber
2 Squadron	Canberra B.Mk 20	Butterworth	Light bomber
38 Squadron	Dakota	Changi, Kuala Lumpur	Medium-range transport
RNZAF			
14 Squadron	Venom FB.Mk 1	Tengah	Fighter, ground-attack
75 Squadron	Canberra B.Mk 2	Tengah	Light bomber
41 Squadron	Dakota C.Mk 3, Freighter 170	Changi, Kuala Lumpur	Medium-range transport

Also deployed during the Confrontation were Avro Vulcan bombers like these eight examples photographed while lined up at RAF/RAAF Butterworth. (Albert Grandolini collection)

month, which amounted to 900 killed and wounded for the loss of 700 MRLA.[77]

The end of 1948 saw the measures implemented by the civil and military administrations beginning to have an effect. The army had been strengthened with more personnel in country allowing the police to defend static sites, meaning that the army could now undertake jungle operations against the MRLA. The Min Yuen had hoped to make Pahang a secure area allowing the MRLA to launch attacks against opposition forces. This proved not to be the case when in August 1948 they were forced out of the area.[78]

The withdrawal into the jungle also created problems for the MRLA. Incidents dropped markedly. At the end of 1948 attacks from jungle camps were at 50 a week but from February 1949 until December of the same year, they dropped to 26. MRLA forces showed a marked reluctance to attack well defended areas or where the element of surprise was nullified. In contrast to this army forces were able to mount punitive incursions into the jungle, succeeding in killing 618 MRLA for a loss of 229 personnel during 1949. In a series of actions beginning with Operation Gargoyle, the Cameron Highlands, Perak and Selangor were cleared, succeeding in halting MRLA forces in the area. This was followed by operations Ramillies, Blenheim, Spitfire and Sarong against No. 5 Regiment MRLA between April and July, forcing the MRLA northwards but a pincer movement from Perak and Kedah, operations named Pintail, Widgeon, Pathfinder and Overall halted their retreat.[79] Between April and September 1949 operations Triangle, Snow White, Lemon, and Plunder were carried out in south-west Pahang, northern Negri Sembilan and Selangor against No.1 Regiment MRLA, killing 37 of the 45 MRLA posted there.[80] The Min Yuen, in an attempt to stem the tide of waning support, rebranded itself as the Malayan Chinese Association in an effort to gain support from non-committed Chinese, though eventually reverting back to the MRLA. They also changed tact in recruiting Malays who were disenchanted with the current government, becaming known as No 10. Regiment; however, from its inception it was constantly attacked by army and government forces so that within a year, it had ceased to exist.[81]

Min Yuen and MRLA dreams for Malaya were given a glimmer hope through communist successes in China, Korea and Indochina between 1949 and 1950, along with the subsequent recognition of Mao Tse-tung by Britain and Ho Chi Min by Russia. This also hampered army and government forces' hopes of swaying non-committed Chinese who were now reluctant to help them in case they were singled out as being collaborators should the MCP gain power in Malaya.[82]

Operations against the MRLA continued for the remainder of 1950 with mixed success. It was not until 1951 that the actions of the MRLA would reach a high point both politically and militarily. Malaya would see far reaching changes while Britain saw a change of government with the Conservatives restored to power. A series of successful attacks by the MRLA, coupled with the MCP changing tact, saw doubts being sown within Malaya that the MCP might be on a winning footing.[83]

Three key events stand out in 1951, the MCP Central Committee issued a series of directives which changed how the party would function, placing less emphasis on military tactics against the

The Westland Whirlwind was a British, licence-built – but much uprated – version of the US-made Sikorsky S-55/H-19 Chickasaw. In Borneo, it was deployed for moving troops and supplies, and for patrolling. Together with the similar Wessex, it was the true 'workhorse' of the RAF. (Albert Grandolini collection)

general populace, coupled with developing the party's base within the masses. From now on both military and political aspirations were given equal prominence in the MCP's campaigns.[84]

The second event or incident which was to cast a shadow over the end of 1951 was the assassination of High Commissioner Gurney. Third was the failure in some areas of the new resettlement villages. Some had to be bulldozed while others were closed due to poor living conditions and security, and subsequent attacks by the MRLA.[85]

The events leading up to the assassination of the High Commissioner began on 6 October 1951. Gurney and his wife, along with his private secretary, left Kuala Lumpur to travel the 65 miles to Fraser's Hill (a small hill resort) for a weekend break. The convoy consisted of a police Land Rover, the High Commissioner's Rolls Royce, a radio van, a private car driven by the Attorney General, and a police armoured scout car. The radio van experienced technical difficulties forcing those inside it to transfer to the scout car. However, the time taken by personnel moving from one vehicle to another meant that the scout car had to travel flat out to make up time and distance to the rest of the convoy. By this point the High Commissioner's car reached a one-way section on the road to the resort. A small platoon of guerrillas had set themselves up in a prime ambush point. Upon seeing the open-topped Land Rover and the Rolls Royce – too tempting a target to ignore – they opened fire with Bren guns, hitting the Land Rover and injuring the police within the vehicle. These police were woefully ill prepared for such an attack and were armed only with side-arms and bolt action rifles. Gurney for his part, and perhaps to draw fire away from the Rolls Royce with his wife and secretary, stepped away from the car and tried to get to a culvert, but was shot and killed before reaching it. The attackers then proceeded to climb down to remove any weapons they could find but were met by the rapid approach of the scout car which was armed with a Bren gun and proceeded to lay down supressing fire.[86] The aftermath of Gurney's death resulted in increased military activity near the scene of the crime. The nearest Chinese village of Tras was removed entirely without regard to who was innocent or guilty. This opened up a greater gap in relations between the Chinese populace and government forces. The British government had to act to fill Gurney's position and at the same time cull other personnel who were either not up to the task or had ruffled too many feathers in Malaya.[87]

A month after Gurney's death, the MRLA inflicted its highest number of casualties on the security forces. It also looked like the government's emergency policy was floundering with no one in power to take it forward. Briggs had retired and died shortly afterwards. Meanwhile the Colonial Secretary, Oliver Lyttelton, had received numerous complaints about Gray, the Police Commissioner, and he was also removed from his post, quietly retiring after a meeting with Lyttelton. The British government now needed to recruit personnel who would suppress the MRLA and take Malaya forward to independence.

1951–1952, The Year of Change

The problems besetting the both the Malayan and British Governments in 1952, were also very similar to those the MCP would experience. For the MCP some high-ranking officials would question the party's direction, and some would defect to the government side and undermine the MCP's political hierarchy. While the Malayan government needed a replacement for Gurney, the Police Commissioner, and other staff who had either resigned or retired. Whoever these replacements were, they needed to get the plans back on track quickly and see it to its logical conclusion.

MCP Troubles

For the MCP, it was a change of policy that was to highlight the cracks. The rank and file had begun to harbour resentment against those higher up within the party who still had pretensions for the finer things in life while the rank and file were having to give up everything for the party. It was this political infighting that was slowly tearing the party apart. One of the major critics of the path that the MCP was taking was Lam Swee, former Vice President of the Pan Malayan Federation of Trade Unions, a leading light in the South Johore Regional Committee and Political Commissar of the 4th Regiment, MRLA. He had been very critical of the MCP but surprisingly was not shot but was placed under house arrest and ordered to rethink his views and admit his mistakes. Swee was also branded as an internal spy. Swee, seeing the writing on the wall, escaped from the jungle, evaded his captors, and surrendered to government forces in June 1950.[88] The MCP had to also hold itself accountable for the execution of Siew Lau, one of the MCP's more forward thinking and notable theoreticians. Lau had become very vocal on the direction that the MCP was taking, arguing that burning buses, slashing rubber trees and indiscriminate shooting at trains was alienating the very people they were hoping to recruit. Lau ultimately sealed his fate by arguing that in the present environment the MCP should rebury its arms, take stock of where they were, and learn from other successful communist countries. Once better educated they could then recommence the fight against the government. The MCP Central Committee did not like this train of political thinking, going as far as to send a representative who demanded that Lau stand before the Central Committee and retract his views. Lau and his followers declined their offer. Lau was subsequently betrayed by a friend after asking the Malacca Special Committee for funds to leave the country. Lau, his wife Sow Wah, and Siew Ping were incarcerated and placed in isolation. The MCP, fearing perhaps that Lau would become a new figurehead taking

Prime Minister Winston Spencer Churchill. (Albert Grandolini collection)

Lieutenant General Sir Gerald Templer, later Field Marshall. (Albert Grandolini collection)

followers with him, was shot along with Wah and Ping. Once news of Lau's death got out, many began to question the MCP Central Committee's actions, alluding to it being little more than terrorism to destroy peace and order.[89]

New Governments in Britain and Malaya

Britain in 1951 was in some respects worse off than Malaya. Food rationing was still in place, being more strictly controlled than in Malaya. Churchill, taking stock of what the Conservative government had inherited from the previous Labour one, came to the conclusion that the country was near to bankruptcy, implementing a series of cutbacks including his and the cabinet's wages.[90] Along with the Emergency, Churchill also had troubles in the Middle East, Egypt had taken steps to nationalise the Suez Canal, while in Panmunjon peace talks were ongoing to end the Korean War. Against this backdrop, Churchill focused on Malaya, stating that 'If Malaya goes all the Far East goes.'[91]

While the MCP was reeling from political infighting, the Malay government was also rethinking its strategy after Gurney's death as tensions and anti-Chinese feelings were running high within the country. With many wanting swift action in response to such a heinous crime, the new Conservative government in Britain needed to appoint a new High Commissioner. This could not be rushed, but time was not on the government's side. The new Colonial Secretary, Oliver Lyttelton, after visiting Malaya decided that a general was required to fill the role. The list of potential candidates included Field Marshal Sir Bernard Montgomery, General Sir Brian Robertson – Commander-in-Chief Middle East Land Forces (CinC MELF) – and Field Marshal Sir William Slim. Both Slim and Robertson declined the post, while the British national press had already placed Montgomery into the role. Lyttelton also saw other high-ranking officers before offering the role to Lieutenant General Sir Gerald Templer, who was at the time General Officer Commanding-in-Chief Eastern Command. Templer was flown to Canada to see Churchill who, after meeting him offered Templer the post.[92] Churchill advised him to 'ask for power, go on asking for power and then never use it.' Templer, however, was given the most comprehensive powers ever given to a British colonial official.[93] While Templer was making plans for his new post, some Conservative and Labour MPs still viewed Malaya as the 'dollar earner for the whole of the Commonwealth' while another back bencher wanted Britain to remain in Malaya permanently as an equal partner. This, however, would not happen as Churchill reaffirmed self-government for Malaya in March 1950.[94]

In 1951 Lyttelton visited Malaya prior to Templer's appointment. The Malayan government was also undergoing a period of change. On his arrival in Kuala Lumpur, Lyttleton was met by del Tofo, the Chief Secretary, who was now the Officer Administering Government. Briggs had retired, while the Director of Intelligence Sir William Jenkin was asked to resign along with the Police Commissioner Gray. Malayan politics were also in a transitional phase, UMNO (United Malay National Organisation) had lost its leader Dato Onn who had moved to the Independence for Malay Party. It was against this backdrop that Lyttelton met with UMNO and the future Prime Minister Tunku Abdul Rahman, whose first question to the Colonial Secretary was whether self-government still on the cards, to which the empathic answer was yes.[95]

After these meetings had concluded Lyttelton returned to Britain and set about the task of replacing those who had retired, resigned or had been murdered. Lyttelton was also worried about the state of Malayan politics and perhaps Templer's appointment came at an opportune time. Templer arrived in Malaya in February 1952. His arrival was greeted with mixed feelings: although Templer was occupying a civilian post he seemed more at home in his general's uniform. Some viewed this as a start of positive military action. Others – Malcolm MacDonald among them – were not happy with this appointment and especially with the fact that Templer had no previous Malayan experience.[96] One of the first appointments made by Templer was that of Deputy High Commissioner. This was assigned to Donald MacGillivray who oversaw the day to day running of Administration and the Federal Legislative Council until a speaker was appointed. Again, this met with some resistance as some Sultans and senior Malay politicians thought that a Malay should have been appointed but deferred to the Colonial Secretary's choice of MacGillivray.[97] On the military and operational front MacGillivray's counterpart was General Sir Robert Lockhart, the Deputy Director of Operations and along with Templer, was on friendly terms with GOC Malaya, first Major General R.W.

A Soviet-built BTR-50 amphibious armoured personnel carrier in service with the Indonesian *Korps Komando* (*KKO* or Naval Commando Corps). Significant quantities of equipment from the Eastern Bloc were ordered by Indonesia in the late 1950s through to the mid-1960s. (Albert Grandolini collection)

Urquhart and later Major General Sir Hugh Stockwell. The Colonial Secretary also secured for a fixed term of one-year A.E. Young, the Commissioner of Police for the City of London. Young restored the low morale within the police, travelled extensively in country and managed to inspire confidence in those he met. What was also important is that all these men had a good working relationship with Templer. With new personnel in place the task could begin to get the Emergency back on track. Templer in many ways was the hammer needed to crack the Malayan nut.

Templer early on realised that the civil service in Malaya was suffering from low morale, and the red tape and buck passing that prevailed needed to be stopped. He did what he could to improve pay, housing and the terms and conditions of employment. Templer also did not suffer fools and was quite prepared to cull where necessary, to get the job done.[98] Unlike his predecessor, Templer had erected a perimeter fence around the official residence of King's House and always had an armed guard whenever he travelled. He also managed to impress the local population by visiting villages and *kampongs*, discussing their problems and, if possible working out a solution that suited them.[99] It has been argued that Templer was driven by his own personnel philosophy of how to conduct a counter-guerrilla campaign. Two points stand out. The first was that it was wrong to separate peacetime activities of the government from the Emergency. He stressed that all departments should play an active role submitting whole heartily to making the Emergency their first concern. The second was the often quoted 'Hearts and Minds' which also played a major part in the Confrontation. In Templer's case his main concern was that the general population, not just the higher echelons, were all treated equally. This marked a significant change by the government, which was widely welcomed by all sections of Malayan society.[100]

The Battle for Hearts and Minds

The Colonial Secretary gave a radio broadcast before he left Malaya. In his speech Lyttelton prioritised the police and Home Guard that would be retrained and reorganised, as covered previously. Templer set about this task and coupled this and the expansion of the administrative arm of the government to deliver the social services he saw as necessary to draw civilians away from the MRLA. As for the police, Templer and Young had a good working relationship, allowing Young to reorganise as he saw fit. When Young left Malaya in 1954, the police were in a better state of preparedness and the move from a paramilitary force to one based on civil police duties. Young and Templer introduced Operation Service to show Malays that the police were servants of the people and whose job was to protect all members of the communities; it was a resounding success.[101] By March 1953 manpower of the police was at 71,000, of which 41,000 were special constables and 4,000 were constables. By 1954 the number had declined to 54,000 personnel. It was still also plagued by the lack of Chinese policemen who were still hesitant to join the ranks. When Young returned to Britain in 1954 Templer replaced him with W.L.R. Carbonnell, a Malayan-trained officer, to lead the police.[102]

The Home Guard also benefitted from Templer's involvement with the appointment of retired Major General E.B. de Fonblanque in 1952, with a remit to build an organisation separate from the police and capable of defending the rural population against attacks. After some trepidation, the Home Guard were armed with shotguns and proved to be a force not to be taken lightly. Templer also took an idea suggested by a leading Chinese politician, Leong Yew Koh, who proposed to implement the Kinta Valley Home Guard; miners in the area would pay for full-time armed Home Guard to provide security for the area.[103] The Home Guard proved to be very beneficial. The Malay Home Guard had 100,000 members and defended 2,000 settlements, while the Chinese Home Guard by 1952, had 50,000 personnel with units in every new village; in 150 new villages they were given complete responsibility for the defence of their community.[104]

Templer realised that intelligence and the gathering of information still needed to be improved. It was starting to improve but, in Templer's eyes not fast enough and, the information gleaned was not always reliable. Templer seconded the second in command

A British-built, turbine-powered development of US-made Sikorsky H-34 Choctaw, the Westland Wessex entered service in 1961 and was deployed in significant numbers by naval air squadrons of the Fleet Air Arm. (Albert Grandolini collection)

In addition to being used to transport troops and supplies, the Royal Navy deployed its Wessex helicopters for fire-support and armed them heavily in this role as can be seen from this frontal view. This example is armed with pods for 68mm unguided rockets on the outboard hardpoints, and French-made Nord Aviation SS.11 guided anti-tank missiles. (Albert Grandolini collection)

of MI5 for a year. His remit was to reorganise and expand the Special Branch within the police. A Director of Intelligence was also appointed, to provide information on the MCP's strengths, weaknesses, and strategy and the attitude of various groups towards the communists. A Special Branch Intelligence was also created, while other areas were improved.[105]

The army was not left out as Templer's changes swept through Malaya. Large scale sweeps of the jungle that had been previously used in the vain hope that they might catch the MRLA off guard were scaled down. In doing so, better results were starting to be achieved. This was in part due to the police now being better informed of MRLA comings and goings, this was then relayed to army headquarters, who could then pinpoint areas to be patrolled and cleared. As a result, more contacts were made, allowing the army to prune MRLA personnel while also improving the morale of soldiers posted into the jungle.[106] The use of helicopters – initially Whirlwinds – allowed forces to be quickly moved to hot areas and also meant that casualties could be quickly evacuated back to hospitals, and improved confidence. During the Confrontation helicopters were used on nearly a daily basis.

The Korean War had been very lucrative for Malaya and Templer was quite prepared to dip into these reserves to reform the civil administration. The government's total revenue had risen from $235.5 million in 1948 to $725.4 million in 1951.[107] The total cost of Defence, Police and the Emergency rose from $82 million in 1949 to $287 million in 1952, representing a 350 percent increase.[108] Between 1953 and 1954, like most countries, Malaya experienced a recession but weathered it better due in part to the profits made from the Korean War. Cutbacks were made but it did not impact overall on the forces and personnel now in place.

As the Hearts and Minds approach slowly began to succeed it was also in some cases necessary to use the stick to bring home a point or to handle a situation. Templer was not averse to using the stick when required. In April 1952, 12 men and an Assistant District Officer (ADO) were killed in an ambush near Tanjong Malin. This attack caught the headlines as the ADO was Michael Codner, a hero of the famous wooden horse escape from a German POW camp. Templer visited the village and getting no cooperation from the village elders imposed a 24-hour curfew and reduced the rations for men, women and children. This was a normal occurrence but what was not was a questionnaire, used to find out what the villagers knew about the communists in the area, to be filled out and placed in a secure box. When Templer went through the data a number of suspects were arrested. The curfew was lifted, rationing was returned to normal but more importantly the village fully cooperated with the government.[109] Another village was not as lucky as Tanjong Malin. When a Chinese Assistant Resettlement Officer was shot in the village of Permatang Tinggi, the residents refused to divulge any information to the authorities and were punished by all being interned in a detention camp while the village was razed to the ground.[110]

The Royal Air Force followed in similar fashion, and began arming its Whirlwind helicopters with SS.11 anti-tank guided missiles – two of which can be seen installed on the outrigger of this example, photographed while underway on a patrol, low over the jungle canopy. (Albert Grandolini collection)

Getting Results

As seen in Tanjong Malin, when information was used effectively results happened. Templer decided to offer rewards of cash payments for information which according to Noel Barber were 'truly staggering.'[111] On 1 May 1952, the cash reward for Chin Peng was $250,000 alive and halved if killed; Members of the Politburo equated to $200,000, again halving if killed; with $120,000 for Regional Committee Secretaries, dropping to $4,000 for Branch Committee Members and $2,000 for regular personnel.[112] It was preferable to try and capture personnel as it was hard to question them when they were dead. Templer was aided in this by C. C. Too from the Psychological Warfare Department, Lam See and Bob Thompson. Thompson reworded the directive to make it more attractive to relatives of MRLA and Min Yuen to help their relations to defect.[113]

The results were immediate with many handing in their arms and defecting to the government's side. Indeed, one husband and wife who turned themselves in were so surprised by how they were treated that they returned to the jungle and brought back 11 more MRLA personnel, netting a shared reward of $12,875.[114] One area which Templer and his forces had no control over was the Thai border, which the MRLA and civilian communists used with impunity. Young reached out to his Thai counterpart but was met with apathy from their side.[115] Working away in the background, Special Branch had started to get better results on MRLA locations and the movements of personnel. One innovative way of obtaining information was to cleverly refurbish old radios then allow them into general circulation. These radios would eventually end up in a jungle camp. Once the persons using these radios tuned to a specific broadcast such as Radio Malaya or Peking, the radio would emit a homing signal which allowed Special Branch operatives to pinpoint these camps allowing the army or police to attack them. Special Branch had also managed to infiltrate the courier service which carried messages between camps, or from Chin Peng, or regimental commanders. This had been made possible by recruiting double agents who allowed the documents to be copied. This had to be carried out very carefully as the messages were sealed in a specific way, though Special Branch managed to replicate this and did not arouse suspicions.[116] Special Branch had begun to act as a very professional unit under Young's leadership, going from strength to strength.

Another nail in the coffin of the MCP/MRLA aspirations was citizenship. Templer, after seeing the results of the Kuala Lumpur municipal elections, saw that Tunku Abdul Rahman was the politician on the up. Rahman would eventually become the leader of Malaya and upon its independence Malaysia. The question of citizenship as a means to take the fight out of the MCP could now be addressed. Malcolm MacDonald had already laid down the groundwork and it was now just a matter of getting politicians and Sultans on board. The Tunku enthusiastically endorsed the plan, while Templer then spoke with the Sultans. They agreed, realising that if they opposed the idea, it would be years before the country gained its independence. By 14 September 1952, 1,200,000 Chinese – 60 percent of the population in Malaya – and 180,000 Indians had become Malayan citizens, along with many British children who had been born in the country.[117]

1951 saw the MRLA/Min Yuen achieve a high rate of victories but this was to be turned around in 1952, when the security forces gained the upper hand. A series of high-ranking leaders either surrendered or were killed. Over a period of a few months, Chin Peng saw 1,502 men lost, including four prominent leaders. The first of these was Manap the Jap who was shot by a Gurkha patrol while walking along a jungle path. This was followed a few months later when the 'Bearded Terror of Kanjang' was killed: National Servicemen from the Suffolks walked into his jungle camp and after a brief fire fight managed to kill the Bearded Terror and his compatriots. It was not by chance that the Suffolks had found the camp but was based on intelligence information obtained, which led to the camp and enabled the successful operation to neutralise the threat. Shorty Kuk was shot and beheaded by his own men after bragging about the reward on his head of $200,000. Kuk's death was kept quiet for a few months while Bob Thompson went through the papers which had been found in Kuk's haversack. These proved to be interesting as they showed a growing rift between the MRLA and the Min Yuen. Min Yuen personnel were up in arms over the fact that the MRLA could flee back to the jungle to regroup while the Min Yuen had to bear the brunt of the government attacks.[118] The final blow to the Min Yuen was the defection of Ming Lee, who after months of evading capture by the South Wales Borderers walked into a police station and surrendered. When questioned by Colonel Richard Miers of the South Wales Borderers why, Lee answered 'I've given up working for those Communist people they're no good. And besides you are winning anyway.' Lee also added that Miers' company had been giving Lee's group a hard time.[119]

There were parts of the country that the MRLA/MCP held where security forces were still unable to make inroads. One such area was the village of Yong Pen in Johore. The MRLA were so blasé about their activities that the planters in the area were delivered the underground communist newspaper. The planters quite disparagingly called Yong Pen: one-third red, one-third pink, one-third afraid.[120] One MRLA leader, Goh Peng Tun, had so perfected the art of ambushes that Chin Peng circulated details of Tun's methods to other MRLA forces. But the days of mounting a successful ambush and slipping back into the jungle had passed. Tun on two occasions failed in attempts to ambush cars and planters. On one occasion the personnel subjected to the attack managed to survive and on the second occasion the armoured car driven by a 14-year boy pushed a dumped car off the road and continued on its way.[121] Even potentially easy targets such as railways were becoming harder to attack. Security Forces were now much quicker to respond, while the trains themselves were better protected. The Green Howards also patrolled stretches of the rail lines in two armoured petrol-powered locomotives.[122] This had a knock-on effect as the MRLA losses mounted; the killer squads were often leaderless and retreated further into the jungle meaning that attacks on civilians and security forces dropped. This also meant that food was harder to come by and even Central Committee Members were found wanting for food.

By the spring of 1953, perhaps realising that the writing was on the wall, Chin Peng decided to continue directing the uprising from across the border in Thailand. It was in all probability an admission of defeat on Peng's part: many of his compatriots were either dead, imprisoned or defected to the Governments side. Templer himself had also decided to leave Malaya: he realised that if he stayed on he ran the risk of him becoming a father figure for the country, which he thought was unwise as Malaya approached independence.[123] The war, Templer argued, was nearing its end. It was now time for the politicians to take over, something he thought he was unable to do. Churchill was against Templer leaving Malaya but finally saw what he meant and being the wily old politician, he realised that if Templer left the chances that Malaya would stay in the Commonwealth were pretty good. One more nail hammered into the MCP's coffin was an idea by Bob Thompson to use former MRLA personnel as a special force called the Special Operational Volunteer Force (SOVF) to convince those in the jungle to lay down their arms and surrender. The volunteers served for an 18-month period after which they returned to civilian life. The force was billeted in police compounds. Thompson also put forward the idea of dropping pamphlets into the jungle to persuade those still left there to surrender, and along with the SOVF this proved to be very effective in thinning the ranks of the MRLA.[124]

Merdeka

As Malaya headed towards independence, sporadic fighting was still ongoing although not at the levels of 1951–1952. By 1955, the estimated strength of MRLA personnel had dipped to 3,000 from previous highs of between 8,000–10,000 men.[125] More and more areas were now being declared white, meaning they were clear of communist control or infiltration. Along with MRLA forces being squeezed into smaller areas of defensible jungle, this brought about

Tunku Abdul Rahman speaking at the Independence Day celebrations on 31 August 1957. (Albert Grandolini collection)

The British High Commissioner at the Independence Day celebrations on 31 August 1957. (Albert Grandolini collection)

Amongst the first RAF aircraft deployed on Operation Ale – the British intervention in reaction to the revolt in Brunei – were three Beverley C.Mk 1 transports of No. 34 Squadron. They helped fly a battalion of Gurkhas from Singapore to Brunei Town and Labuan on 8 December 1962, and then maintained a steady flow of men and supplies throughout the Confrontation. This example, seen at Changi around the time, wore the serial XM104. The insets show details of another Beverly C.Mk 1 of this unit: XS260, which had the dark blue cheat line extended along the fuselage and down the black anti-glare panel. All had their top sides painted in white, and other parts in high-speed silver finish. (Artwork by Tom Cooper)

Hard on the heels of the RAF Beverly C.Mk 1s followed several of the then still relatively new Lockheed C-130A Hercules transports of No. 36 Squadron, Royal Australian Air Force. They first brought reinforcements into Brunei Town and Labuan, and then helped maintain the flow of supplies. Left in highly polished bare metal overall, the Australian Hercules of the time had a cheat line in dark blue applied along the centre fuselage, and a large unit insignia on the fin in between the serial and the fin flash. (Artwork by Tom Cooper)

The third transport type to see most action early during Operation Ale was the Bristol Freighter 170. Operated by No. 41 Squadron, Royal New Zealand Air Force, several of these became involved not only in rushing reinforcements from Kuching and Changi to Brunei Town and Labuan, but also in the following air bridge from Singapore. As usual at the time, RNZAF Freighters were left in bare metal overall, with white applied from around the cockpit down the upper side of the central fuselage. In addition to NZ5904 illustrated here, another example confirmed as being involved in the Borneo Stand-off was NZ5910. Like other aircraft involved, they quickly began showing heavy wear and the influence of the local climate. (Artwork by Tom Cooper)

Another transport type to see action early during the Brunei revolt was the Handley Page Hastings C.Mk 1. Several examples from No. 48 Squadron, RAF – including serial TG569 illustrated here – became involved in flying in reinforcements from airports in the Singapore area in December 1962. Through the following year, they were also deployed to drop supplies for troops underway deep in the jungles of Borneo where there were next to no roads. Hastings of No. 48 Squadron were painted in high-speed silver finish overall, with the upper half of their fuselage in white, and a cheat line in dark blue down the full length of their fuselages. A black serial was always applied on the rear fuselage, and its 'last three' repeated on the fin. (Artwork by Tom Cooper)

Home-based at RAF Seletar from 1929 until 1942, and from 1949 until 1959 (when it moved to RAF Changi), No. 205 Squadron was the longest-serving squadron of the RAF in Singapore. Unsurprisingly, the unit's moto became *Pertama di Malaya* ('First in Malaya' in the Bahasa language). As of 1962, No. 205 was operating Shackleton MR.Mk 2 maritime patrol aircraft, but when the revolt in Brunei erupted, its aircraft were used to transport reinforcements from Singapore. As usual for the 1960s, the Shackletons were painted in dark sea grey overall, with the top of the fuselage in white. The squadron number was applied in red, outline in white on the rear fuselage, right in front of the serial number (WL745 in this case), which was repeated on the undersides of the wing. (Artwork by Tom Cooper)

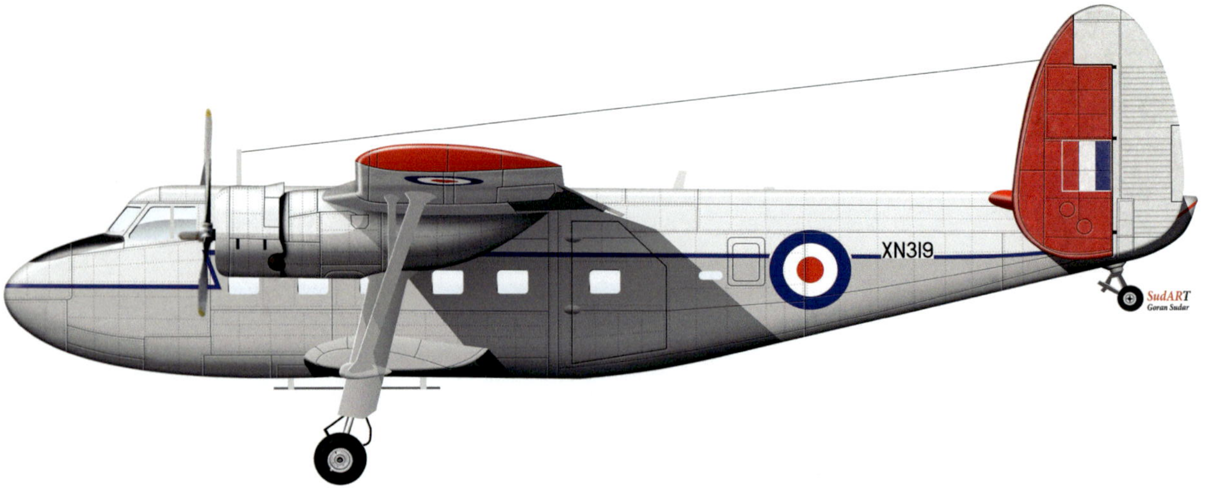

Home-based at RAF Seletar, in Singapore, Scottish Aviation Twin Pioneer CC.Mk 1s of No. 209 Squadron, appeared in their peacetime livery early during the Borneo Stand-off. This consisted of white on top surfaces, and high-speed silver finish on undersurfaces, with a blue cheat line in between, and most of their fins and outer wing panels painted in red. The type proved highly successful thanks to its short take-off and landing performance which enabled it to operate from strips as short as 900ft/275m and was thus intensively deployed for local transport and liaison work. (Artwork by Goran Sudar)

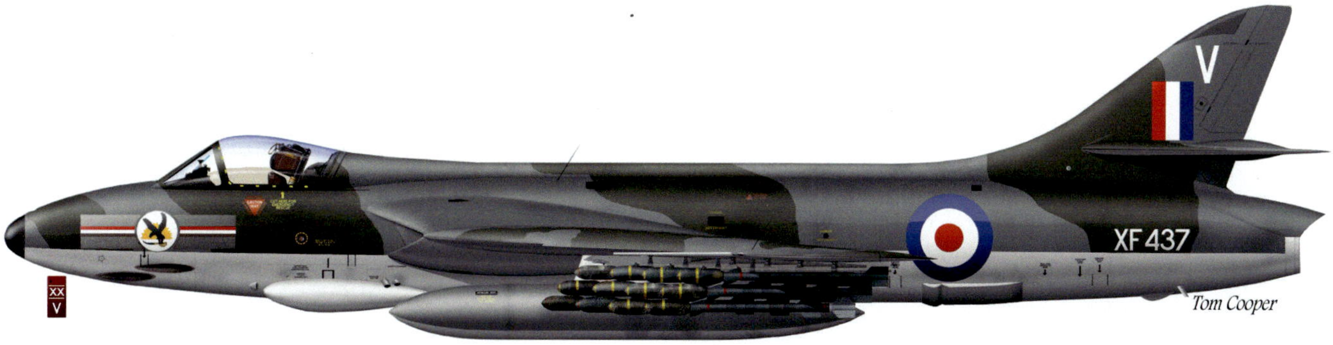

The second combat type operated by the RAF to reach the scene were Hawker Hunter FGA.Mk 9s of No. 20 Squadron. Originally dating back to 1915, this squadron served with RAF Germany before being disestablished in 1960. A year later, it was re-established at RAF Tengah in Singapore, and equipped with Hunter FGA.Mk 9s that wore the standardised camouflage pattern in dark grey and dark green on upper surfaces, and high-speed silver finish on undersides. No. 20 Squadron's rectangular marking was applied on the nose flanking the eagle emblem applied on a white circle, while nose-wheel doors were painted in red with a white XX on the top portion and the aircraft's letter code below. (Artwork by Tom Cooper)

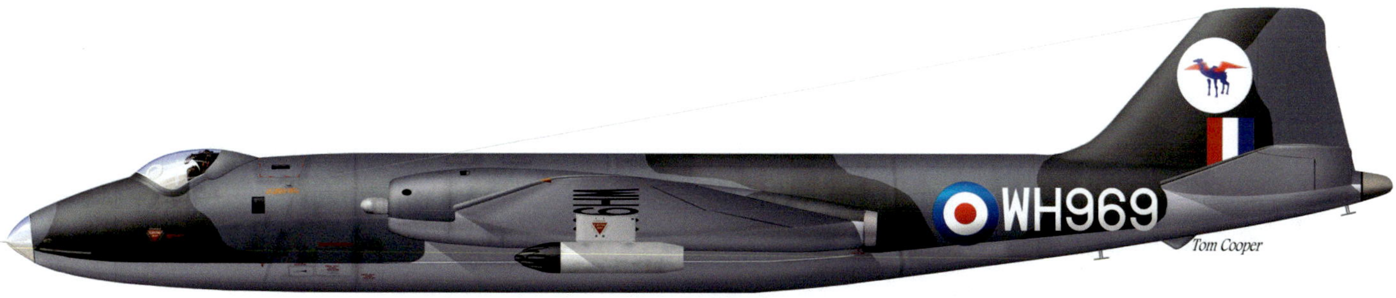

No. 45 Squadron, RAF, was home-based at RAF Tengah and one of two ground-attack units of the Far East Air Force (FEAF). In 1962, it was re-equipped with Canberra B.Mk 15s – a variant deployed by the Near East Air Force and FEAF only, and thus rarely seen in Europe. Based on the B.Mk 6, this version was optimised for low-level attack and equipped with two underwing pylons capable of carrying a 1,000lbs bomb or a Mighty Mouse pod for 37 2.75in/68mm unguided rockets. This is a reconstruction of the B.Mk 15 serial number WH969, forward deployed to Labuan on 8–9 December 1963, and then flown by Wing Commander Pedder in one of the first armed reconnaissance missions over Sarawak. The jet was painted in dark sea grey and dark green on upper surfaces and sides, and high-speed silver on undersurfaces. (Artwork by Tom Cooper)

This is a reconstruction of the Bristol Belvedere HC.Mk 1 serial XG473/E, from No. 66 Squadron, RAF, that crashed in the Trusan River Valley, near Long Merarap, Sarwak, on 4 May 1963. The crash site was found by a patrol from 22 SAS, which concluded that all nine of the crew and passengers – including Flight Lieutenants A. P. J. Dobson and D. R. E. Viner, RAF, and Majors R. H. D. Norman and H. A. I. Thompson from 22 SAS – had perished. Subsequent investigation concluded that the loss was caused by a cable failure that resulted in the loss of yaw control and prompted the RAF to ground its entire Belvedere fleet for two months. As usual for the period, the helicopter was in high-speed silver overall, with white on the upper half of the fuselage. As far as is known, it wore no unit insignia. (Artwork by Tom Cooper)

Home-based at RAF Tengah, No. 60 Squadron was a re-equipped with early-mark Gloster Javelin interceptors in 1961 and received its first four Javelin FAW.Mk 9s (including the example illustrated here) from No. 64 Squadron in November 1963. Once the Indonesian forces began operating aircraft in support of the guerrillas in Borneo in early 1964, No. 60 and No. 20 Squadrons formed the Borneo Jet Force, forward deployed at Kuching and Labuan. The camouflage pattern of No. 60 Squadron's Javelins consisted of dark sea grey and dark green over, and high-speed silver finish on undersurfaces. No. 60 Squadron's crest (the head of a *markhor*/antelope) was usually outlined in the colour of the flight (red for A, blue for B, and green for C Flight). The typical configuration included two 230-gallon drop tanks and a pair of Firestreak air-to-air missiles. (Artwork by Tom Cooper)

Theoretically, the Indonesian Air Force of 1962 was lavishly equipped with Soviet-made MiG-17s, MiG-19s and MiG-21 interceptors, Il-28 light- and Tu-16 medium bombers, and a miscellany of other aircraft and helicopters of similar origin. However, the force was already heavily involved in the confrontation with the Netherlands over West New Guina/Papua, and short on qualified pilots. When mobilised to support the rebellion in Borneo, some of its fliers had to switch from MiGs to older, though proven as reliable, North American P-51D Mustangs. Most of these wore camouflage in olive drab on top surfaces and sides, and a large shark-mouth insignia on the nose surrounded by dark blue, and the crest of 3 Skvadron under the right side of the cockpit. The undersides were left in bare metal overall. In addition to the six wing-mounted 12.7mm Browning machine guns, they could also be armed with four rails each for two unguided 88mm rockets. (Artwork by Tom Cooper)

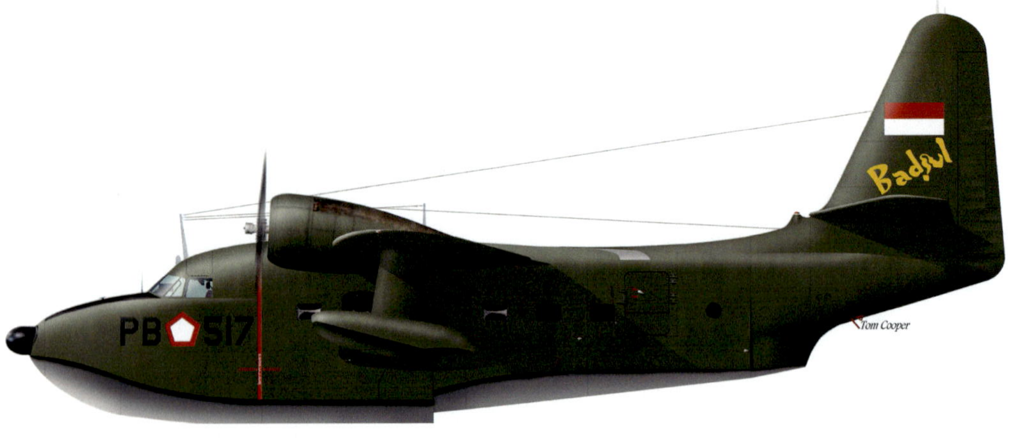

Because of continuous rebellions, several coup attempts, and the Confrontation with the Netherlands over West New Guinea/Papua, the majority of Indonesian combat aircraft of the period between the mid-1950s to mid-1960s were painted in olive drab overall. This appears to have been the case with the small fleet of AURI Grumman UF-1 (also HU-16A or SA-16A) Albatross amphibians, as shown in the main artwork. Alternative reports indicate that the original livery in dark grey (FS35164) was extended overall, covering the white that had been applied on the top fuselage and parts of the fin (as shown inset). Serial PB517 is known to have received the large title 'Badal' on the fin, apparently applied in yellow. Nominally, the Indonesians deployed their Albatrosses for search and rescue purposes, however, at least as often they were used for tracking the movement of Royal Navy warships. (Artwork by Tom Cooper)

A dog handler from 1st/2nd Battalion Royal Green Jackets, shown in standard Jungle Greens and armed with a Sterling sub machine gun. 7.62mm Self Loading Rifles were used alternatively. Generally, dogs were Labradors, who were semi-successful in flushing out insurgents in house-to-house searches and in the jungle. (Artwork by Anderson Subtil)

Gurkhas had been stationed in South East Asia since the Malayan Emergency and excelled in jungle warfare and cross-border incursions. This Rifleman is shown dressed in Jungle Greens with a black beret, Type 58 webbing with Kukri (the traditional Gurkha curved fighting knife), and armed with an L1A1 SLR. (Artwork By Anderson Subtil)

Scouts were primarily recruited from the inland tribes, of which the Ibans were just one. While some wore boots and shorts, as shown here, the majority were bare-footed or wore flip-flops or sandals. Initially armed with shotguns, they eventually received .303 Lee Enfields, here in the Jungle Carbine version; many still carried blowpipes and machetes ('parangs'). (Artwork by Anderson Subtil)

The Border Scouts were trained by the SAS and the Gurkha Independent Parachute Company, and often deployed along the border while commanded by Gurkha section commanders. They were issued with standard Jungle Greens and black berets. The cap badge in the upper right corner is that of the Sarawak Rangers, and including a crossed Kris and *parang ilang*, and a crown. The service title and the Toucan insignia were worn on the shoulders. (Artwork by Anderson Subtil)

Present in the area since the Malayan Emergency, and then due to their country's obligation as a member of the SEATO pact, Australian military advisors were issued with Jungle Greens and the khaki fur felt or slouch hat that was always worn with a *puggaree*. (Artwork by Anderson Subtil)

Uniforms issued to the MRLA guerrillas were modified from stocks left behind by the British at the end of the Second World War. Most were armed with Lee Enfield .303s, and received the Type 68 webbing, slightly altered to better suit the jungle environment. (Artwork by Anderson Subtil)

The first unit of the British Army equipped with armoured cars and deployed to Borneo was B Squadron of the Queen's Royal Irish Hussars (QRIH) equipped with Saladin and Ferret armoured cars. The QRIH arrived on 9 December 1962, together with the troops of 42 Commando of the Royal Marines, 1st/2nd Gurkha Rifles, and the Queen's Own Highlanders. Usually painted in dark green overall, the Saladin (shown here) weighed 11 tonnes and was armed with a 76mm gun, and two Browning .30-calibre M1919A4 machine guns. (Artwork by David Bocquelet)

The second unit equipped with Saladins and Ferrets to reach Borneo was C Squadron of the Queen's Royal Irish Hussars, which disembarked at Kuching on 15 December 1962. Its troops saw action almost immediately while securing the roads to Serian and Simangang. This Saladin had not only the tactical insignia of the QRIH in the form of a red and yellow quadrant, but also a pair of Kukris in white (indicating affiliation with the Gurkhas). Many others received personal names, usually starting with 'D'. (Artwork by David Bocquelet)

C Squadron, Queen's Royal Irish Hussars arrived in Borneo by April 1963 in time to counter the first of the long-awaited Indonesian incursions. Like A and B Squadrons, in addition to Saladins, the unit was equipped with Ferret armoured cars, each of which had a crew of two and was armed either with a .303 Bren or a .30 Browning machine gun. The Ferret illustrated here belonged to the fourth unit of this type to see action on Borneo during the Confrontation with Indonesia: H Squadron, 5th Royal Tank Regiment. (Artwork by David Bocquelet)

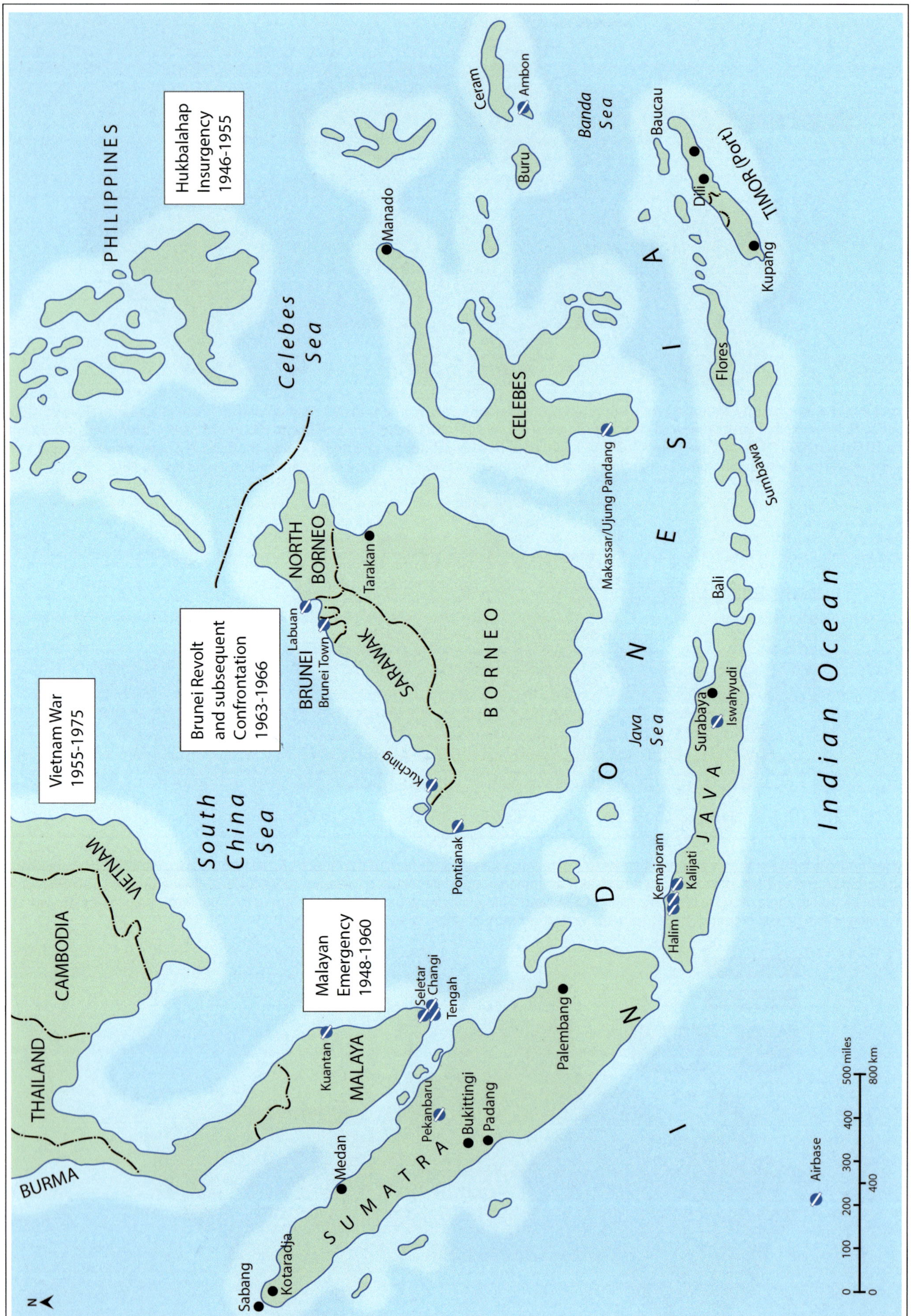

A map of South East Asia in the 1950s and 1960s, showing the major crises in this part of the world and the most important air bases used by by all parties to the conflict during the Borneo Stand-off. (Map by George Anderson)

Tunku Abdul Rahman speaking at Independence Day celebrations and to Radio Malaya on 31 August 1957. (Albert Grandolini collection)

a change of tact from Chin Peng who offered a negotiated end to the Emergency. The new Alliance government under Tunku Abdul Rahman were unsure of the feelers being sent out by Peng. The Tunku's government was prepared to offer an amnesty to the MRLA as a means to shorten the Emergency.[126] The Tunku also offered to meet Peng and discuss terms of ending the Emergency and the amnesty terms. The resulting talks were held in a small town of Baling on the Malay border with Thailand between 28 and 29 December 1955.[127] The MCP representatives consisted of Chin Peng, Rashid Maidin (of the Malay Nationalist Party), and Chen Tian (head of MCP's Central Propaganda Department). The Malay government's representatives included Tunku Abdul Rahman, Dato Sir Cheng Lock Tan (leader of the Malayan Chinese Association), and Mr David Marshall (Chief Minister of Singapore).[128] Talks were held over a period of two days with many areas being discussed. One key area that both sides agreed on was the ending of hostilities, but the talks soon broke down over other demands as the gulf was wide and insurmountable. One sticking point was the recognition of the MCP as a legitimate party.[129] The Tunku had come to the conclusion that it might prove impossible for communism to coexist alongside what Tunku viewed as the Malayan way of life.[130] This created a deadlock with the Tunku unwilling to change his position, while Peng was not empowered to accept the terms of the amnesty. One positive result of the talks was an agreement signed by both sides which stated that as soon as the Federal government obtained complete control of internal security and local armed forces, the MCP would end hostilities, lay down its arms, and disband its armies.[131] This was the highlight of the talks as they broke down shortly after. When Malaya gained independence in August 1957, the MCP was still defiant stating that 'the maintenance of British and Commonwealth troops in Malaya after independence was proof that the government had not obtained control of internal security.'[132]

It was post-independence Malaya that saw a near collapse of the MRLA. After Merdeka Day (the Malay term for Independence Day) MRLA/MCP realised that all the races within Malaya had celebrated its independence. Pressure being applied by the security forces resulted in 500 personnel surrendering and the MCP was unable to fill the void left by these men and women. This allowed the government to carry out mopping-up operations. The remainder of the MCP under Chin Peng stayed on the Thai side of the border.[133] The MCP had become in many respects a tiger with no teeth though it has been argued that the MCP never really disbanded until 1989 when communism was finally defeated.[134] For Malaya this was the start of a period of peace within the peninsular, it was not until 1962 that Malaya would again see armed conflict on its borders.

3 POLITICS IN THE REGION POST-1957

In order to better understand Britain's role in the Confrontation, it is necessary to consider the thinking in London in creating the new state of Malaysia so soon after Malaya had gained its independence in 1957. The creation of Malaysia was a military response as well as a way for Britain to divest itself of its remaining colonies in South East Asia, but at the same time holding onto the large military base in Singapore, thus allowing Britain to remain a global power.[1]

As seen during the Emergency, the ethnic population of Malaya was a mixture of Malays, Chinese, and Indians, while Singapore's population was predominantly Chinese. Across the South China Sea Britain still had interests in Borneo; North Borneo and Sarawak where the population was a mixture of Malay, Chinese, Dyaks and Kadayans. The British also had a protectorate, the Sultanate of Brunei, which will be discussed in detail in due course.[2]

The Malayan Idea

On 27 May 1961, at a lunch held in Singapore, the Malayan Prime Minister Tunku Abdul Rahman, in a seemingly throw away comment suggested that a closer understanding between the peoples of Malaya, Singapore, North Borneo, Brunei and Sarawak was needed. The Tunku continued with this thread by implying that these countries could be brought closer together in political and economic cooperation.[3] This statement was a change of tact: the Tunku, had previously been opposed to any union between Malaya

The Royal Australian Air Force acquired and operated a large fleet of Lockheed P2V-5 and P2V-7 Neptune maritime patrol aircraft from the early 1950s well into the 1970s. A detachment of Neptunes – including the P2V-5 (later P-2E) serial number A89-309 (nicknamed Pussy Galore) seen here – were prepared for deployment during the Malayan Emergency in 1955 and in 1959–1960, but this was apparently cancelled. (Albert Grandolini collection)

and Singapore.[4] These remarks seemed to galvanise political leaders who saw the creation of a Greater Malaysia as a means to satisfy their various needs.[5]

The Tunku, being an astute politician, could see that if these colonies were to merge it would tip the balance of the population, making it more Malay-centric rather than the predominantly larger Chinese population, split between Malaya and Singapore. Indeed, Malcolm MacDonald had been championing the Grand Design which was similar to what the Tunku had suggested. Also, if these remaining colonies were to merge with Malaya, it could forestall any claims by Indonesia and the Philippines on the Borneo colonies.[6] However, the Colonial Office opposed the idea, arguing that it would take years before Sarawak and North Borneo were at the same level as Malaya politically, economically and educationally.[7]

Although Britain had granted independence to Malaya, it still had military obligations; firstly to the country and secondly, to the defence of the region. The 1957 Anglo-Malayan Defence Agreement (AMDA) committed Britain to defend Malaya's borders. In return the Malayan government allowed Britain to retain forces in country, thereby enabling Britain to fulfil its Commonwealth and international obligations.[8] In the event of war breaking out in the area, Britain still had to maintain its SEATO obligations, which allowed Commonwealth and American forces to protect the area. This and the idea of a Greater Malaysia all hinged on retaining the large military base in Singapore, which if refused or declined was a deal breaker in London seriously undermining Britain's commitments to SEATO, Australia and New Zealand.[9]

The military base in Singapore was becoming a problem that needed to be addressed quickly. The Tunku had gone on to suggest that after the merger the Singapore base could no longer be used for SEATO operations and could only be used for the defence of the Commonwealth. This would make Britain's SEATO obligations impossible to fulfil.[10] The Tunku went on to say that North Borneo, Sarawak and Brunei could be brought into the Malayan Federation quickly as additional states. Why was the Tunku trying to rush this through? The answer was population demographics. If Singapore joined with Malaysia this would increase the Chinese population to the point where it would outnumber Malays. This was unacceptable to the Tunku and other Malay political leaders.[11] However, if Sarawak, North Borneo and Brunei were to join their combined populations of mainly non-Chinese populace it would negate any Chinese dominance within the newly established state of Malaysia.[12] Singapore was also a political problem for Malaya. The Tunku was still hesitant to incorporate Singapore into Greater Malaysia. Indeed, the British High Commissioner in Kuala Lumpur, Sir Geofroy Tory,

The leader of Singapore, Lee Kuan Yew. (Albert Grandolini collection)

reported that the Tunku showed no signs of softening and went as far as to state that 'the bulk of the Chinese in Singapore were incapable of ever adopting a truly Malayan viewpoint and therefore of being assimilated safely into the federation.' He continued 'they (the Chinese) will never be Malaya's friends in a thousand years.'[13] The Tunku's reservations about Singapore were soon borne out, when a political crisis erupted on the island. The party that held political power, the People's Action Party (PAP) under the leadership of Lee Kuan Yew,[14] was under increasing pressure from a newly formed party consisting of its own disillusioned former members.

The Royal Navy's aircraft carrier HMS *Eagle* was deployed in the Borneo area from January to April 1965. This photograph shows a Fairey Gannet AEW.Mk 3 of NAS 849 (B Flight) ready to be catapult-launched from its bow. Visible overhead is a Handley Page Victor bomber of the RAF. (Albert Grandolini collection)

This new party was *Barisan Socialis* (Socialist Front), anti-colonial, and had become the main opposition party.[15] Lee feared that in the forthcoming elections it was a real possibility that *Barisan Socialis* would gain a majority and thereby scupper any chances of merging with the Malayan Federation. Both London and Kuala Lumpur feared that *Barisan Socialis* was under the influence of communist infiltrators and if successful in the elections a communist party would control Singapore. Lee could rely on some of the smaller parties to push forward the merger but if the wind changed these parties could topple the government and force a general election if the opportunity arose.[16] PAP was weakened with only 26 seats in the 51 seat chamber, leaving the government open to votes of no confidence by opposition parties.[17] So if the merger was to take place it had to be done quickly.

While Singapore was sorting out its own political problems, overtures were being made to the political parties in the other territories. Lee, in a meeting held in Singapore, met representatives from Sarawak and North Borneo, while other meetings were held in Kuala Lumpur with Donald Stephens from North Borneo who had been an anti-federation advocate.[18] Datu Mustapha, who was the main Malay-Muslim leader in North Borneo, and Datu Bandar, the head of Party Negara, Sarawak, after talks with the Tunku, all decided to get behind the idea of unified Malaysia.[19] The only country that seemed to be dragging its heels was Britain. This raises the question what Britain's views were of a unified Malaysia.

London's Response

London's cautious approach was one of financial outlays, and government and army departments throwing their hats into the ring to slow the formation of Malaya. Lord Selkirk, the UK Commissioner for Singapore and Commissioner General for South East Asia from 1959–1963, on hearing the Tunku's idea of a Greater Malaysia, suggested that the government should either drag its feet or appear to be taking over the initiative.[20] Was London right in being cautious? The governors of Sarawak and North Borneo, Sir Alexander Waddell and Sir William Goode had strong reservations about a Greater Malaysia and erred on the side of caution, suggesting that it would take years to get both states ready to join Malaya. They also raised concerns about being absorbed by Malaya, with no regard for local autonomy to protect the indigenous population.[21] The Colonial Office also shared this view and persuaded the Tunku to delay any statements on the merger with Malaya. In May 1960, the Colonial Office, Foreign Office and Commonwealth Relations Office, thought that the merger with Malaya in the long term was a good idea as it would forestall any attempts by Indonesia, the Philippines or China to influence or lay claims to these smaller territories.[22] However, the Tunku's growing impatience with London came to a head in June 1960 when at the Commonwealth Prime Ministers' Conference the Tunku sought face-to-face talks with British representatives. Lord Perth, the Minister of State for Colonial Affairs, was willing to accept a Federation of Malaya, Singapore and the three territories. Nonetheless Perth understandably gave the impression that Britain was neutral, but Lord Selkirk in an about face now supported the Tunku's plan.[23] Selkirk went as far as to recommend to the Foreign Secretary, Selwyn Lloyd, that the plan was the best way forward for long term stability in the area. However, the Colonial Secretary, Ian Macleod, was more cautious, pointing out that the Borneo territories showed no inclination for independence and the majority of the people were happy to remain under British control. Macleod suggested that Britain should adopt the attitude of benevolent neutrality towards the Tunku's plans.[24]

Militarily speaking, Britain had a large footfall within the area, with Singapore being the largest military base and housing the Royal Navy's Far East Fleet, a naval dockyard, three military airfields, command and control centres, an army base with workshops, supply depots, stores and a hospital. All this allowed Britain to maintain a large military presence for military and political functions.[25] Macleod argued that if Britain was to adopt the Grand Design allowing Singapore to merge with Malaya, it would end Britain's rights to use the base on Singapore, and become dependent on negotiated treaty rights with an independent state, which would be less secure.[26] Besides, Britain could no longer maintain the status quo in Singapore as political developments were making this impossible. Along with this was the speed with which European countries were allowing colonies in Asia and Africa to gain independence. Britain had in 1957 allowed Singapore limited self-rule but the ever-present shadow of communism still hung over the island and if they managed gain a political foothold on power then holding onto the base would be tenuous at best.[27]

The Cost of Maintaining a Military Presence

Another factor which Britain had to take into consideration was the financial cost. If all the territories merged, then it might be financially cheaper to maintain a military presence in South East Asia. Since the end of the Second World War the economy and sterling had struggled to return to pre-war levels. This had caused the Treasury to look at the cost of maintaining a force in South East Asia. The Chancellor, Derick Heathcoat-Amory, had been telling the cabinet since 1960 that Britain faced a balance of payments shortfall, and this was in part due to military spending.[28] Harold Watkinson, the Defence Minister, in July 1960 highlighted the fact that military overseas expenditure for 1960–1961 would amount to £200 million which would increase to £235 million in 1961.[29] The Prime Minister, Harold Macmillan, asked Watkinson to look at ways of cutting military expenditure. Macmillan's thinking was that in the event of a war in South East Asia, Britain would have the backing of the numerically superior forces of the United States. So, if the military forces stationed in the area were to be downsized, this force could be used to mount police actions and maintain or cover potential hot areas. This force in theory would consist of the Commonwealth Strategic Reserve allowing a pull-back of other military forces.[30]

However, the Chiefs of Staff (COS) had other ideas. In 1961 their revised plan for the area did not in fact show any downsizing of forces stationed in Singapore and the surrounding area. The COS claimed in order to maintain military effectiveness it could afford to lose a divisional and brigade headquarters, and two army major units such as infantry battalions, armoured regiments, field artillery regiments, air defence batteries, Royal Marine commando units and Royal Engineer field squadrons. This could be offset by transferring a commando unit from Aden to Singapore.[31] The COS argued that the ongoing security issues within Singapore necessitated keeping a large force on the island, fearing that otherwise the government of Singapore would fall. Watkinson was disappointed with what the COS had put forward, and the Defence Committee reluctantly accepted the plan in January 1961.[32] Regardless of what Britain wanted to do, it was still tied to the area by SEATO and treaties for the protection of Malaya.

Not to be deterred, the Tunku continued to press for the amalgamation of the states, along with the inclusion of Singapore, to counter any communist threats from within the island. Whitehall in the meantime had set up the Greater Malaysia Committee (GMC), whose initial findings had advised caution over the Borneo territories, and yet argued that achieving a Greater Malaysia should be regarded as an aim of British government policy.[33] Both London and Kuala Lumpur regarded Singapore as a powder keg ready to blow, and if it did, the political landscape would change for the worse. The GMC also recommended constitutional safeguards that allowed the territories some degree of self-government.[34] A visit to these territories nearly backfired when the Tunku enthused about Brunei joining but was somewhat disparaging of Sarawak and North Borneo. This raised the fear that these states would be dominated by either Brunei or Malaya although this was not the case.[35] The Cobbald Report, which had been convened to look at the Borneo territories joining Malaya, was quite positive of the merger.[36] While the politicians debated the pros and cons of the creation of Malaysia, the average person on the street needed to know what was going on; propaganda was introduced to explain the government's thinking and was used with various degrees of success. The propaganda was semi-successful depending on where you resided. In Singapore, Greater Malaysia was marketed quite vigorously as the island population was opposed to the idea of joining Malaya. While in Brunei, the Sultan seems to have been apathetic to the idea of marketing Greater Malaysia, allowing Party Ra'ayat to voice its opposition to joining Malaysia. The sheer amount of propaganda material that was sent to Singapore and smaller states was overwhelming. The government had a clear field, as none of the opposition parties could think of a scheme to counter the creation of a Greater Malaysia. By 1963, the

Harold Macmillan addressing the UN General Assembly. (Albert Grandolini collection)

Duncan Sandys, UK Colonial Secretary. As Minister of Defence he authored the notorious 1957 White Paper that radically shifted UK defence policy from a focus on manned aircraft to guided missiles. (Albert Grandolini collection)

A Bristol Belvedere from No. 66 Squadron, RAF, dropping off supplies to a *kampong* (village). Forward deployed at Labuan, Kuching, and Seletar, the unit was involved in Borneo from December 1962 until February 1967. (Albert Grandolini collection)

supporters of the Malayan scheme outnumbered its opponents in each of these states.[37]

Meanwhile in London, Duncan Sandys had replaced Ian Macleod as Colonial Secretary. Sandys had come from the Ministry of Defence and Macmillan had faith in Sandys to make Greater Malaysia happen.[38] As will be seen later, Sandys' work with the Tunku and Lee was set against the backdrop of the pressure being applied through military actions by Indonesia within Borneo while trying to create Malaysia.[39]

The Indonesian, Filipino and US Views

Indonesia initially had not taken much interest in the formation of Malaysia. The newspapers in Djakarta had not reported it and the government had for all intents and purposes feigned disinterest. This was due in part to Indonesia's ongoing claims of sovereignty over West Irian which was still under Dutch control.[40] One of the main Indonesian political parties, *Partai Komunis Indonesia* (PKI), at first did not see the formation of Malaysia as something that it should oppose. This was to change in December 1961, after a meeting in Djakarta of the far left Partindo party which had members in Brunei and Malaya and was opposed to the formation of Malaysia. Its paper *Bintang Timur* put forward a neo-colonialism interpretation of Malaysia along with a charge that the Tunku's aim was to oppose Indonesia. This statement seems to have galvanised the PKI's Central Committee which between 30 and 31 December issued a resolution denouncing Malaysia as a form of neo-colonialism to strengthen the hand of imperialism in South East Asia while implementing SEATO activities against Indonesia.[41] The PKI would also show solidarity with the oppressed peoples of Sarawak, North Borneo, Brunei and Singapore who were against the formation of Malaysia. However, the ongoing military actions in West Irian, along with other more pressing problems, for the time being took precedence over countering the formation of Malaysia.[42] This in part allowed politicians to gain support over the ongoing claims over West Irian, especially in the UN.

America had also been drawn into the political mire surrounding West Irian and South East Asia. Having acted as a mediator between the Dutch and Indonesia, this had allowed the eventual transfer of West Irian to UN administration until Indonesia took over in 1963.[43] President Kennedy was eager to foster good relationships with Djakarta, while Djakarta still had reservations about Britain, which had helped the Dutch reoccupy West Irian. Britain had interests within Indonesia and had blocked any attempts by the Dutch to counter Indonesian claims over West Irian.[44] Kennedy, for his part, wanted a quick solution to this as Vietnam and Thailand were more important in America's eyes, and militarily speaking were using a lot manpower; 8,000 in South Vietnam and 10,000 dispatched to Thailand to counter the renewed fighting in Laos during May 1962.[45] Kennedy and Washington did not want to be dragged into another conflict.

Perhaps emboldened by the actions of Indonesia in West Irian, the Philippines was to throw its hat into the ring and in doing so was to muddy the waters around Malaysia even more, arguing that sovereignty of North Borneo should return to the Philippines. This idea was brought forward by President Diosado Macapagal. Macapagal offered no hostility towards the creation of Malaysia so long as North Borneo was returned. The request for talks between Manila and London were politely declined, as officials in London viewed the problem as one Malaysia could sort out once it had been created. London went on to explain to Washington that as long as Indonesia remained disinterested then Macapagal's claim was not a cause for concern in London.[46] Even the Tunku's overtures to mediate in West Irian created problems, leading to diplomatic sabre rattling, and allowing Sukarno time to formulate a plan to provide military aid to anti-Malaysia groups and claim these territories.

However, for the time being it could be argued that Djakarta was playing possum. Dr Subandrio, the Deputy Prime Minister, wished the Malay government well in its endeavours to create Malaysia. Lieutenant General Djatikusumo praised the Malayan scheme, although he changed tact 18 months later, after becoming ambassador in Kuala Lumpur, in line with Indonesian policy of what would become known as 'Crush Malaysia.'[47] Indonesia did not even raise concerns over changes to the AMDA agreement during 1961 or the wording of the new use of Singapore as a base for potential SEATO purposes.[48] It was not until 1962 that the question of the creation of Malaysia was to gain more significance within Indonesia, with critics calling for more decisive action. Ali Sastroamidjojo, chairman of *Partai Nasional Indonesia* issued a statement which kicked the hornet's nest. Sastroamidjojo and his party were too much on the fringes of the government to have any real influence, but his statement started a series of complaints from Kuala Lumpur including that Malaysia might increase the danger of war in the region because its purpose was to give military bases to big powers.[49]

Sastroamidjojo also advocated that Indonesia should not remain indifferent to what was happening in the region so soon after the West Irian campaign.[50] This argument was also continued by the Indonesian Foreign Minister Dr Subandrio in a tetchy interview given in Kuala Lumpur and subsequently published by *The Straits Times*. Subandrio implied that if any bases were to be constructed in North Borneo, Sarawak or Brunei then Indonesia would reply in strength. The reporter either rightly or wrongly assumed that Subandrio meant American bases not British. If a base was built, then Indonesia would respond in kind by allowing a Soviet base to be built within Indonesia to counter this perceived threat. The reporter commented that considering that Indonesia had feigned disinterest in the formation of Malaysia, it was in fact threatened by the formation of Malaysia.[51]

Maphilindo

While politicians from Indonesia and Malaya pointed fingers and sabre-rattled, another idea was put forward to try and derail the formation of Malaysia, or at least slow it down. Or was it to align the entire region and curb the rise of communism? At its centre was Sukarno and this in itself brought its own set of problems.

The idea of a Pan-Malay organisation was not new. As early as the nineteenth century thinkers envisioned a union of Malay peoples encompassing Borneo, the East Indies, Malaya and the Philippines.[52] During the 1930s Malaya Irredenta was adopted by Young Philippines, a nationalist movement of which the future president Macapagal was a member. However, this version also factored in Burma, Thailand and Indochina, making it a larger federation of countries. In 1964, Cambodia expressed an interest in joining what was now being termed Maphilindo. Meanwhile the Philippines also championed the inclusion of Thailand and other mainland states.[53] Indonesia saw itself as the centre of this and pursued the idea.

Premier Tunku Abdul Rahman (left) meets Philippines President Diosdado Macapagal (right) on 10 June 1964. (Albert Grandolini collection)

In 1962, Macapagal, using the pretext of the Borneo claims, suggested the idea of a Greater Malay Confederation comprising Malaya, the Philippines, Singapore, Sarawak, Brunei, and North Borneo. Macapagal left the door ajar for Indonesia to join but this idea did not gather much momentum outside of Manila.[54] As will be seen, in 1963 the area was to be drawn into conflict after Sukarno's outburst of 'Crush Malaysia' at the formation of that state. Macapagal called for leaders to attend a conference held in Manila in an attempt on his part to try and defuse the situation within the area. This had the required effect, with both the Tunku and Sukarno agreeing to meet despite the fact that Sukarno was still sending forces over the border and attacking Tebedu in the Sarawak subdistrict of Serian.[55]

A series of meetings held between 7–11 June resulted in what became known as the Manila Accords. These accords set out that all the countries concerned would share responsibility for the security of the area, and more importantly, without surrendering any portion of their sovereignty.[56] While these talks were being held Britain and Malaya were pressing ahead with the formation of Malaysia with the target date of 31 August 1963, although this was to be moved to 16 September. Sukarno for his part viewed the continuing talks between Britain and Malaya as an affront and continued punitive cross-border incursions. This in turn prompted Sarawak, North Borneo and Sabah to proceed with joining Malaya, as a way of preserving their interests.[57]

Sukarno at one point threatened to walk away from the talks and in a show of bravado only arrived at the ninth hour after informing the US ambassador that he would attend, and with his blessing Maphilindo was created. It was a short-lived endeavour but at the time it was lauded as a success. The US acknowledged its creation and bank rolled it with aid packages to the value of $250 million for Indonesia's economic recovery.[58] This was to backfire with Sukarno siding, at least on paper, with Russia after defaulting on the American loans.

Creation of Malaysia

As already indicated, Malaysia came into existence on 16 September 1963.[59] On paper it had dotted the I's and crossed the T's. However, behind the scenes the many players were manoeuvring their pieces on the political chessboard for the final outcome.

The British had viewed the Tunku's talks in Manila as a failure, perceiving the Tunku as weak in readily giving in to the demands of Macapagal and Sukarno. One British official commented that the Tunku had mucked up the negotiations by taking a position which he

The UN Secretary-General U Thant (left) meets with Norwegian Air Force Lieutenant General Odd Bull at United Nations Headquarters on 14 June 1968. Bull was commander of UNTSO peacekeeping/observer mission in the Middle East between 1963 and 1970. (UN Photo)

knew Britain would not accept. Sandys had also sent a message to the Tunku warning that no amount of plebiscites would alter Sukarno's basic hostility to Malaysia.[60] Another outcome of the Manila Conference was the UN becoming involved in the formation of Malaysia. U Thant (1909–1974) the Secretary-General of the UN was asked to provide an independent and impartial role in the formation of Malaysia. U Thant's representative Alfred Mackenzie, head of the UN Technical Aid Mission in Manila, was tasked with leading a team to look into the Malaysia question.

Duncan Sandys (second from the left) and the future Prime Minister of India Indira Gandhi (third from the left). (Albert Grandolini collection)

U Thant's cable presumably was addressed to Mackenzie, as it is unclear exactly who the recipient was. On the question of Sabah, North Borneo and Sarawak, UN General Assembly Resolution 1541 could be implemented to ascertain if a referendum might be undertaken in the countries that intended to merge with Malaya.[61] The idea of a referendum was out of the question in the Tunku's mind but a visit by the Secretary-General or his representative was acceptable.[62] From the Indonesian viewpoint they hoped that Resolution 1541 would be invoked to push Malaya and Britain into a corner. However, the parameters of the resolution had been met with elections being held in Sarawak and Sabah on the question of joining Malaya.[63]

In the event U Thant eventually sent four cables. The second was worded very similarly to the first cable. The third, however, gave the Tunku some political leeway while the first two had put the Tunku on the defensive, the idea of a referendum was off the table. This new cable allowed agreement without a referendum and allowed the continued creation of Malaysia.[64] For Sukarno and Macapagal it was a case of saving face as the referendum plans had failed. For his part Sukarno hoped that if the Tunku had been forced to delay the formation of Malaysia because of the issues of self-determination, it would have potentially created a wedge between Malaya and Britain, this however, proved not to be the case.[65]

United Nations Involvement

The outcome of the toing-and-froing between the United Nations and the delegates in Manila was that a United Nations ascertainment team would be sent to Borneo. The team on its own would have been fine, but initially the team would be joined by an unspecified number of Indonesian, Philippine and Malayan observers.[66] This in itself was to prove problematic, as Indonesia and Philippines spent two weeks arguing over the number of observers and their status. London meanwhile was growing more and more impatient with the lengthening delays, finally telling U Thant that only two observers from each country could accompany the UN team. This ultimatum was rejected out of hand by Jakarta and Manila, to which London grudgingly raised the quota to four. The original figure of nine had been rejected out of hand and Jakarta still thought that the number of four personnel was insufficient.[67] To settle this once and for all U Thant intervened raising the number to four observers and four junior executives or clerical assistants. This was deemed acceptable by both Djakarta and Manila; even London seemed happy with the outcome, although very suspicious of the Indonesian and Filipino personnel. London had cause to be sceptical as it transpired Jakarta, in a blatant attempt of subterfuge, tried to use higher ranking personnel many of whom had intelligence backgrounds. Manila also tired this and like Jakarta was found out. The deal breaker for London was when Indonesia wanted to fly their personnel into Borneo on an Indonesian plane: the Foreign Office on 26 and 27 August rejected the teams from both countries and refused to grant flying rights.[68]

It also transpired that London's cause for concern about the Indonesian's intentions was borne out. A military attaché in Jakarta had managed to obtain minutes of a meeting held between Subandrio, General Abdul Nasution, the Indonesian Minister of Defence and Magenda, the Chief of Intelligence Indonesian Combined Forces Staff. This information was relayed to London: it outlined that large sums of money should be used to disrupt the UN's work while trying to win over the Borneans.[69] Britain feared that this would, if successful, hamper the formation of Malaysia. Eventually the observers were cleared but they were a full week behind the UN team and so any chance of igniting support for joining Indonesia had passed.[70]

With the UN teams undertaking their work, a new problem emerged: the date for the creation of Malaysia. While the UN were visiting Borneo, London had to maintain an air of confidence so that Borneo, and more importantly Singapore, did not waiver and withdraw from the talks. To keep this on track, a new date for the creation of Malaysia needed to be set, and quickly. The Tunku himself was hesitant is setting a firm date, preferring a more flexible approach: to London, and especially Sandys, this smacked of appeasement to keep Indonesia happy. Sandys was subsequently sent to Malaya to bring the Tunku back in line and in the meetings that followed the Tunku was treated more like an underling than a head of state. However, Sandys' pressure worked, and a new date was set to which the Malayan cabinet agreed: 16 September 1962.[71] Britain had already decided to press ahead with creating Malaysia even if a date for its creation had not been set, and regardless of what U Thant's team found in Borneo, even though Washington thought it was not wise to publicly acknowledge this intention.[72]

Lee Kuan Yew (left) at an awards ceremony. (Albert Grandolini collection)

Harold Wilson (left) and Lee Kuan Yew (right) outside Downing Street. (Albert Grandolini collection)

Singaporean Poker

London and Kuala Lumpur had enough problems to worry about with the United Nations team in Borneo and trying to second guess what Jakarta and Manila would do next. Lee decided to up the ante and demand more concessions from London and Kuala Lumpur, and brought brinkmanship to a new level. It also took Britain's eye from what was going on between Sukarno and Macapagal. Lee's intent was to play political poker to see who would blink first. Firstly, he called for early elections in Singapore, confident that his party would beat *Barisan Socialis*. Secondly, it would place him in a stronger position to demand more from Kuala Lumpur and London. If this failed, then Lee would withdraw Singapore from the Malayan plan and declare its own independence on 12 September 1962, four days before Malaysia was to come into existence.[73]

In Britain's eyes, if this came to pass then the idea of a little Malaysia and an independent Singapore comprising of a large Chinese population was a step too far. Indeed, in case Lee's threat proved real plans were drawn up to take control of Singapore, arrest Lee and take over the key areas to keep Singapore running. This plan would also safeguard the British base on the island. As Lee now held all the cards, London and Kuala Lumpur met for discussions and decided to agree to Lee's terms. This left a bitter taste in the Tunku's mouth after the berating he had received from Sandys to set a date for the creation of Malaysia, and now had to give ground to Lee to keep the dream alive. The Tunku now had an intense disliking for the Commonwealth Secretary over this and the earlier meetings.[74] Although there was some light in the murkiness, the UN team's findings showed that the majority of the population in North Borneo and Sarawak supported the creation of Malaysia, although both Jakarta and Manila contested the findings. However, U Thant endorsed the findings paving the way for the creation of Malaysia.[75]

Malaysia came into existence on 16 September 1963. It had been a difficult transition hampered by outside forces. Sukarno's ongoing plans to disrupt and continue military operations did not cease and he would turn his attention to upsetting the stability in the area by continuing cross-border incursions into Sabah, North Borneo and in aiding the uprising in Brunei.

4
BRUNEI REVOLT, 1962–1963

After the ending of the Emergency in Malaya a period of peace descended onto the area. Malaya was continuing to push towards full independence with no formal ties to Britain except for trade and military defence agreements. It was not until late 1962 and 1963 that the area would once again become embroiled in what initially started out as an insurgent uprising but developed into a full-scale confrontation. The latter was mainly between Malaya and Indonesia, which viewed Malaya's expansionist plans as a threat to its sovereignty and an affront to its charismatic leader President Sukarno, who some argued had the same agenda.[1]

Background to the Revolt

The seeds of what would become known as the Confrontation began in Brunei, when a small-scale uprising threatened to overturn the Sultanate, resulting in British troops being airlifted into the country from Singapore. The revolt was quickly suppressed with few casualties, but it needs to be examined to better understand the origins of the Confrontation.

Brunei is a small state of 2,226 square miles, located on the north-west coast of Kalimantan or Borneo, with considerable gas and oil reserves, and is ruled by a Sultanate. The British arrived in the country in 1839, when James Brooke landed and proceeded to wrest control away from the Sultan and become known as the White Rajah. The country itself was never under full British control. The subsequent discovery of oil and gas in the 1920s allowed the Sultanate to become extremely wealthy. By the 1960s, due in part to the wealth generated by oil and gas profits, Brunei had initiated free health-, education- and social-welfare services to the population and had low rates of taxation. In 1959, Britain, which was slowly decolonising in Asia and Africa, allowed Brunei to achieve self-

Sultan Omar Saiffudin (1914–1986), the ruler of Brunei from 1950 to 1967, seen at the time of the revolt. (Albert Grandolini collection)

The last White Rajah of Brunei, Sir Vyner Brooke, with his wife Rani Sylvia Brooke. (Albert Grandolini collection)

government, with a constitution being written up, and elections held in 1962. These free elections were won by *Parti Rakyat Brunei* which opposed the Sultanate, seeking full democratic rights without any influence from the Sultan. This notion, however, was rejected and it was here that the seeds of revolt were sown.[2]

The Formation of *Parti Rakyat Brunei*

The formation of *Parti Rakyat Brunei* did not happen as a response to the Sultan's proposals of elections. The party had been formed in the 1950s under the leadership of A.M. Azahari, a 34-year-old of Malay-Brunei decent who as a child had been sent to the East Indies by the Japanese. It was here that the young Azahari dreamed of a new future for Brunei.[3] Subsequently abandoning his veterinary studies, during the Indonesian Revolution he joined one of the many terrorist cells. By 1950 he had relocated to Singapore but was still travelling to Brunei starting a umber of – mainly unsuccessful – businesses. Azahari was still championing Brunei's independence, which led him to being jailed twice by the British and subsequently classified as an undesirable. As Azahari's family had some influence with the Sultan this made him more problematic as, if he had the ear of the Sultan, then it might be possible to promote his brand of politics.[4] As if to prove Britain's hidden agenda within Brunei, Azahari asked to form a company known as the Brunei Film Production Company. It had one simple remit; to highlight the injustice of British law. Initially the Sultan expressed an interest in becoming a shareholder but was persuaded against it. In January 1953 another attempt to form the film company was put forward, with a petition being presented to the British Resident, J.C.H. Barcroft, to reconsider the application. Azahari was at the head of the deputation alongside his brothers and a large crowd of followers. Initially the gathering had been approved by the State Treasurer E.Q. Cousins. However, the Resident was subsequently informed that the gathering was illegal. Upon informing Azahari of this, the latter retired to a house owned by his father not far from the Resident's office to sit and wait for a meeting to discuss his petition. Azahari was subsequently arrested along with his brothers after being coaxed outside to discuss his petition.[5] By 1956 Azahari was bankrupt and turned to politics full time.[6]

It is conceivable that in later life Azahari fell under the influence of Sukarno and this may have made him more radical and more determined to control Brunei. Indeed, Azahari has been likened to Brunei's Sukarno.[7] Sukarno for his part did not publish the fact that he or his government supported Azahari's aims. However, if he was to succeed then Sukarno would then take credit for aiding Azahari in his aspirations.[8] In 1956 *Parti Rakyat Brunei* gained official approval, and as such, began to campaign for electoral representation and the creation of a constitutional monarchy for the Sultan. The British however, viewed the party with suspicion and decided to offer no support.[9] In fact the British wanted an alternative to *Parti Rakyat* as a way of dissolving the power base that it was gaining within the country.[10] Steps were taken in 1957 to counter this threat and eliminate Azahari from politics as it was believed that he had close connections with Indonesia and ergo with the Indonesian communists. Special Branch, using British Malayan Petroleum as a front and aided by British intelligence, infiltrated the Brunei People's Party, hatching a scheme to get Indonesia to respond to a fake crisis in North Borneo and then persuade British North Borneo of the advantages of joining Malaya. The outcome of this was that dissidents from within the Brunei People's Party regrouped and formed the North Kalimantan People's Party and its armed offshoot, the National Army North Kalimantan (*Tentera Nasional Kalimantan Utara*, TNKU), under the leadership of Yassin Affendi.[11]

What Britain had not grasped or realised due in part to the lack of reliable information was the depth of support for *Parti Rakyat* within government offices and at grass roots level. The party's membership had risen to 26,000 and encouraged by this Azahari pushed for the return of Limbang District which had been annexed by the White Rajahs. One newspaper asked where next after Limbang? North Borneo or Sarawak?[12] In the face of political turmoil within Brunei, the Sultan pushed back the elections to 1962. This came at the same time that the idea of Malaysia was put forward. However, in Brunei the idea of a unified Malaysia was met with opposition. Why was this? On paper, Brunei was the ideal template for what Malaya was attempting to achieve; the issues of race, language, religion which were problematic in Singapore, Sabah and Sarawak were absent. Malay was the primary language while Islam was the main religion, the British were on board with this idea and even the Chinese endorsed the idea hoping that they would be granted citizenship. However, the Sultan, *pengirans* (the royal family), and the oil interests were less inclined to join as they had political power within the country, while Britain provided the defence of the country. Why should the status quo change?[13] The Sultan went through the motions of joining Malaysia. In a newspaper interview he again reiterated the idea of closer ties with Malaya even going as far as to approve a loan of $100,000 million to the Federation, following up by stating that he would now attend the meeting in London to complete the treaty agreements. [14] As expected, Azahari on the other hand was against it, arguing that Brunei should return to its former glory and should have Sarawak and Sabah returned to them to enable Brunei to reach its goals. Azahari went on to argue that these territories should themselves become a federation with the Sultan as its head.[15]

In an attempt by the Sultan to placate Azahari's party and political aspirations, he appointed Azahari to the Legislative Council in a nominated unelected post, while simultaneously appointing him to a special commission convened to gather the public view on joining Malaysia. This move by the Sultan backfired, as once Azahari was on the council, he attempted to block Malaysia's formation by tabling a series of resolutions, one of which was the return of Sabah and Sarawak. This could have been seen as a move to undermine the Sultan's leadership as if the resolution was not heard then Azahari would take it to the populace of Brunei to hear their views. The Sultan, sensing a power struggle, ordered the defeat of the resolution, then arranged an alternative that made the joining of Malaysia more palatable.[16] All this came about before the first free elections were held in the country. Again, this was a major blow for the Sultan as *Parti Rakyat* swept the board winning 22 of the 23 seats in the elections. On paper at least, Brunei joining Malaya was still on track, while the states of Sabah, Sarawak, North Borneo and Singapore pressed on with their own plans to join.[17]

As mentioned at the beginning of the chapter, August 1962 saw the postponed elections now being held. The parties involved would experience very different outcomes. *Parti Rakyat*'s main opposition was the Brunei National Organization, but this party turned out to be a failure. Despite the elections being put back a year to allow the party to better organise itself, it failed to counter *Parti Rakyat*'s political agenda. When the results of the elections were announced *Parti Rakyat* had secured 54 of the District Council seats, while its opponents had failed to secure any seats or candidates. The win for Azahari's party meant that it now held all 16 elected posts out of a total of 33 in the Legislative Council.[18]

Were the election results and the subsequent victory of *Parti Rakyat* a show of opposition to the Sultan's plans to join Malaya? Perhaps yes: Azahari was anti-Malayan and was against the British involvement within the country. If Brunei was to join, in his view there would be no change: the conservative nature of the Sultan would continue coupled with the British still in the area. Even worse, Brunei might have to spread its wealth amongst the poorer states, rather than keep it within Brunei and share it with the population once, or if, independence was achieved.[19]

While the political front was being fought, the training of the TNKU had continued unabated, expanding its recruitment base and making ready for whatever would happen in the next few months. Once the dust had settled after the elections, the enormity of what Azahari and *Parti Rakyat* hoped to achieve became apparent. But as they flexed their political muscle they were thwarted either by the Sultan, who would postpone meetings, or the remaining 17 members of the Legislative Council who would oppose what was brought before them.[20] Left with no political avenues to pursue, Azahari had no alternative but to use armed force and seize control from the Sultan.

The Revolt

The revolt did not simply happen. Plans for the revolt, or at least some armed conflict, may have been under consideration for a period of time. When the revolt did break out two things stand out as interesting. The first was how badly organised it was. Secondly, Azahari either knew in advance that it would fail or had distanced himself to a safe country, avoiding any political fallout and to avoid being arrested for the actions of his party. Indeed, Azahari had been out of the country for weeks before fighting broke out.[21] When Azahari left for his trip to Manila, the head of Special Branch in Sarawak, Superintendent Roy Henry, acted quickly, arresting 10 senior TNKU officers in Lawas. They were subsequently transferred to Limbang police station but not before leaking information to a local magistrate that more arrests were imminent. This galvanised the TNKU to bring forward their timetable with the revolt happening on 8 December rather than the original date of 12 December 1962.[22] Britain and Malaya may have been caught napping, but they were aware of an impending uprising in Brunei. However, they seemingly did not fully act on the information supplied. Indeed, even the Tunku tipped off London about *Parti Rakyat*'s intent to start a peoples uprising. Subsequent arrests in Sarawak uncovered documents and uniforms belonging to TNKU.[23] In Lawas, Sarawak, the police in were approached by a grandmother asking them to help release her grandson from the army. The bemused police officer asked which army, to which the grandmother replied the local one, producing a green jungle shirt as evidence. When the police subsequently checked the local markets, it was discovered there had been a 'run' on jungle-green cotton with more being imported in from Singapore.[24] An Affendi had been tasked with raising and training 15 companies of semi-trained volunteers in preparation for the revolt starting in December.[25] So why were military forces caught off guard?

On 8 December 1962 the population of Brunei awoke to find their country in open revolt against the Sultan and Britain. The uprising began in the early hours and the TNKU attacked key areas in Brunei Town and Seria, the centre of the Shell Oil Company installations, while small towns along the coast were also subjected to attacks. Areas of Sarawak and North Borneo, Sibuti, Limbang, Lawas and Weston were also hit by the TNKU. However, the Sultan was not taken prisoner; in fact, the rebel forces seemed quite hesitant about capturing him, while other the administrative areas and some police stations successfully held back the rebels.[26] Azahari, who was in Manila on 'business' when the revolt began, announced on the radio that the Sultan would flip and join their side. Instead, a state of emergency was announced along with a 24-hour curfew and British forces were sent for. What was more damaging for Azahari's aspirations of ruling Brunei, *Parti Rakyat* was banned, while members of the party were rounded up and arrested, culminating with an arrest warrant for Azahari himself.[27] Did Sukarno play a hand in the uprising? Sukarno was staunchly anti-colonialist and the chances were that he could oppose of the formation of Malaysia. One of the largest political parties in Indonesia, the PKI, had openly condemned Malaysia's formation with no dissuading from Sukarno.[28] Although official diplomatic channels assured British politicians that Indonesia had peaceful overtones, Britain was still not convinced. Britain thought correctly that once the West Irian crisis was over Sukarno would turn his attention to the opposing the formation of Malaysia. In a speech broadcast on 1 December 1962, he expressed sympathy for the people of North Borneo who were fighting for their independence.[29] Other evidence of Indonesian involvement in the revolt was gleaned from interrogation reports of TNKU prisoners and other intelligence sources. Britain had early on in the revolt/Confrontation broken the Indonesian diplomatic and military ciphers and could now intercept messages which could then be translated by a Government Communications Headquarters (GCHQ) listening post in Singapore. The US also contributed intelligence, with the Central Intelligence Agency sending reports to Britain, while the US Liaison Officer supplied information to Joint Intelligence Committee (Far East) (JIC(FE)).[30] This not only showed Indonesia's complicity in the revolt but also allowed intelligence departments an insight into political and military thinking within Indonesia.[31]

Military Operations

Once the Sultan had sent for military aid Changi Base swung into action. 8 December saw RAF Beverleys fly out of Singapore heading to Brunei, although initially, flights were routed to an RAF base on Labuan, an island off the coast of Brunei, as it was unclear if the main airfield in Brunei had been taken by insurgents.[32] During the course of the revolt, the RAF, along with RNZAF and RAAF, had a number of aircraft available to carry out various duties:

- No. 20 Squadron, RAF: Hawker Hunter FGA.Mk 9
- No. 34 Squadron, RAF: Blackburn Beverley C.Mk 1
- No. 36 Squadron, RAAF: Lockheed C-130A Hercules
- No. 41 Squadron, RNZAF: Bristol 170 Freighter
- No. 45 Squadron, RAF: Canberra B.Mk 15
- No. 48 Squadron, RAF: Handley Page Hastings C.Mk 2
- No. 52 Squadron, RAF: Vickers Valetta C.Mk 1
- No. 66 Squadron, RAF: Bristol Belvedere HC.Mk 1
- No. 205 Squadron, RAF: Shackleton MR.Mk 2
- No. 209 Squadron, RAF: Scottish Twin Pioneer CC.Mk 1[33]

Additionally, the British Army and the Royal Navy brought in their own aircraft and helicopters, including:

- No. 656 Squadron, Army Air Corps: Auster AOP.Mk 9 & Beaver AL.Mk 1
- NAS 845, Fleet Air Arm: Wessex HAS.Mk 1
- NAS 846, Fleet Air Arm: Whirlwind HAS.Mk 7

Admiral Sir David Luce, C-in-C of British Forces Far East, ordered Plan Ale to be put into action, this allowed Britain to send military aid under the 1959 defence agreement.[34] Plan Ale was a contingency plan put forward by 17th Gurkha Regimental HQ, which allowed a Gurkha contingent to fly a small HQ and two rifle companies, along with detachments of Royal Engineers and Royal Signals into Borneo/Brunei. These would be accompanied by a Military Intelligence Officer who would assist in aiding the restoration of civil law. It was also perceived that no naval involvement would be required unless requested at the alert stage.[35]

The information coming out of Brunei seemed to suggest that the situation did not seem urgent or out of control. By 0400 on 8 December the Gurkha Infantry Brigade was placed on Ale Yellow which meant that the brigade had 48 hours' notice to embark for Brunei.[36] On standby were the Queen's Own Highlanders. However, there were problems gathering up the 1/2nd Gurkha Rifles who were on various exercises and training around Malayan Peninsula.[37] Now these personnel needed to be recalled to Singapore in preparation to fly out to Brunei. The only problem was it was that it was a weekend and even the RAF was caught on the hop when the revolt broke out. Initially Major Lloyd Williams was given overall command of the forces being send ahead to ascertain the lay of the land. This comprised of HQ and C Company flown out on a Beverley, while en route it was confirmed that the main airfield had not been captured by the rebels; a grave tactical error. This meant that Lloyd Williams' force could now fly directly into Brunei as the Beverleys could land there. However, the remainder of the forces which had flown out aboard a Britannia had to fly into Labuan and then be flown into Brunei on aircraft capable of landing on the airfield.[38]

Wessex HAS.Mk 1 helicopters of the NAS 845, Fleet Air Arm, aboard either the aircraft carrier HMS *Albion* or HMS *Bulwark*. In addition to being embarked on aircraft carriers, the squadron operated forward detachments at Kuching, Labuan, Sibu, Belaga, Nanga Gaat, and Simanggang, from December 1962 until August 1965. (Albert Grandolini collection)

Even while troops were being rushed to Brunei there was confusion in the country as to what was unfolding. Azahari's Minister for Economic Affairs, Achmad Zaini, declared that he was the Prime Minister of the Unitary State of North Borneo (NKKU, *Negara Kesatuan Kalimantan Utara)* which had apparently been agreed by the Sultan. Zaini also announced that seven divisions of the North Borneo National Army, consisting of 20,000 men had surrounded Jesselton and a number of other towns. Zaini was misinformed however, and more importantly had no direct contact with either his followers or the rebels, and so had no real idea as to what was actually happening on the ground.[39] The rebellion seems to have miscarried from the outset. When the rebels attacked the small town of Weston on the west-coast railway line of North Borneo, about 60 members of the TNKU armed with seven shotguns, four cigarette-tin bombs and parangs/machetes, attacked the police station, acquired more weapons and advanced further up the railway line towards Jesselton. It was not until the group came under fire and some were wounded that they lost confidence, retreating to their *kampong* and surrendering the next day. This group had believed that they would be bolstered by their comrades from Brunei; this, however, did not occur and other groups experienced similar issues of Brunei rebels failing to appear.[40]

British forces landing at the airfield did so under the cover of darkness, with the rebels seemingly reluctant to attack. From there military personnel made their way to the police station which Lloyd Williams was using as his HQ. By 8 December, Lloyd Williams' force of HQ, C Company and two platoons of D Company were ready for the next phase.[41] The Gurkhas having consolidated their position around the airport meant that flights in and out could now be undertaken without the fear of reprisals. From there it was possible to launch an offensive and retake the capital, meeting little if any resistance from the rebel forces. This was due in part to the fact that the rebels had failed in their objective to raid the police stations and use the ordinance that would have been stored there; most were armed only with shotguns and machetes.[42] This also allowed Lloyd Williams' forces to secure the Sultan who was being held at his palace with minimal TNKU guards watching him.[43]

The Logistics of Moving Inland

On paper it looked like a fairly simple exercise to move inland now that the airfield was secure and the RAF controlled the airspace. However, this was not the case due in part to the poor condition of the road infrastructure and that the revolt occurred during the monsoon season, turning some of the roads into quagmires.

Having thus far met with little if any resistance, Lloyd Williams decided to prioritise two areas to be relived: Brunei Town and the

A Saracen APC bogged down on the roads of Brunei during the monsoon season. The FV603 Alvis Saracen was a six-wheeled armoured personnel carrier shared many components with the Saladin armoured car from which it was derived, though entered service first because of an urgent need for APCs to be used in Malaya. The turret usually carried a Browning .30 machine gun and a Bren gun could be fitted to a ring mount above the rear passenger compartment. (Albert Grandolini collection)

A semi-submerged Ferret being retrieved after a bridge collapse. (Albert Grandolini collection)

Seria oilfields. The Gurkhas were sent to the capital and after a series of short, sharp firefights seemingly secured the capital although this resulted in six casualties, of which two were fatal.[44] It would be a long night for the Gurkha platoons. Intelligence was received that the rebels were going to attack the police station at Panga, using European prisoners as shields. The rebels thought that the police would not open fire and surrender without firing a shot, but this was not the case; the police opened fire resulting in one Eurasian being killed and five other hostages being wounded.[45] This now meant that action was required and fast. Orders were given to Major Lea of C Company, commanding two platoons to fight their way to Seria, secure the prisoners and subdue the rebels. Lea, using two trucks and a Land Rover, proceeded towards Seria. It was as they entered Tutong, a small town on the way to Seria, that they came under heavy fire from the rebel-held police station, the Gurkhas responding in kind. As the patrol went further into the town fighting grew even heavier, and unbeknown to the rest of the patrol the Land Rover containing Lea was hit and crashed into a monsoon drain. The rest of the patrol carried on into Seria oblivious of their officer's fate.[46] Lea and the rest of his men extracted themselves from the monsoon drain, and as they sought refuge in a nearby building were fired upon by rebel forces inside it. A firefight ensued but as the rebels held the high ground/upper floors Lea retreated – after first securing the wireless from the damaged Land Rover – and made for the fish market in the town. Lea and the remainder of his men dug in for the duration, allowing communications to be restored with the Gurkhas who could then backtrack to Tutong. Then with clinical efficiency they cleared the town of any remaining rebels. Some areas proved problematic however, where the rebels held the high ground behind the police station but, ultimately, they waivered and retreated once they came under sustained fire from the Gurkhas. When the dust had settled casualty for the two sides were seven rebels killed, 20 wounded, and 100 captured; one British officer and seven Gurkha other ranks wounded.[47]

With Tutong and Brunei seemingly pacified the operation to relive Seria could now continue. However, the fighting in Brunei Town would suddenly reignite. Lloyd Williams at HQ received intelligence that a rebel was seen crawling up a monsoon drain near a Government Offices Building. Lloyd Williams at once sent a patrol to investigate this report and Lieutenant David Stephens and his patrol was dispatched to the scene. Upon arriving, Stephens led the patrol down the road towards the monsoon drain, suddenly coming under fire from the rooftops of the adjacent buildings. Stephens was killed instantly while the remainder of the patrol returned fire. Meanwhile troops at the police station/HQ upon hearing the firefight proceeded to provide covering fire across open land to the area where the patrol was pinned down. Gurkhas stationed at the HQ then left the building to either secure the

Saladins undergo an impromptu inspection. The circular marking on the turret-side indicate that these vehicles belong to C Squadron, whilst the 'Chinese Eye' insignia on the superstructure (level with the driver's head) was unique to 4th Royal tank Regiment. Note also the L5 105mm Pack Howitzer (British designation for the OTO Melara Mod 56) in the foreground. (Albert Grandolini collection)

British troops of an unidentified regiment patrolling and doing house-to-house searches during the Revolt. They are in shirt sleeve order and have minimal equipment other than their L1A1 7.62mm SLR rifles with bayonets, and Mk III or IV helmets. (Albert Grandolini collection)

Captured TNKU rebels or Indonesian regulars being questioned via an interpreter about their armament equipment. Note the figure on the left (presumably a British or Commonwealth officer) with a pair of long thin pouches for sub machine gun magazines on his belt and wearing high jungle boots. (Albert Grandolini collection)

perimeter or head into town to provide their besieged colleagues with backup. This group was hit by an attack from rebels, intent on taking the police station and capturing those inside. The attack was halted but at the cost of one Gurkha officer wounded, along with four men. one of whom would subsequently die of his injuries.[48]

With sporadic fighting still continuing within Brunei Town, D Company under the command of Major Watterton had landed at the airfield and were now working their way towards Lloyd Williams' HQ. D Company heard fighting but, having no idea of the orientation of the town, were proceeding to what they thought was HQ but was in fact Government Offices Building, from which the rebels were pinning down Stephens' patrol. Watterton halted his patrol and requested radio confirmation so he could orientate himself and was subsequently ordered to attack the building he was heading for, but to compound Watterton's problems his patrol was then fired upon from the rear. Watterton had assumed incorrectly that this was a Gurkha patrol and so disregarded the threat though it was in fact the rebel group who were intent on taking the police station/HQ. Headquarters realised that the chances of D and C Company opening fire on each other was high and ordered Watterton to stay put until sun-up in a few hours.[49]

On the morning of 9 December Watterton cleared the buildings on the eastern side of the town by the river, then headed south towards Brunei Hotel, along the way capturing 14 prisoners who later turned out to be policemen. With all the buildings cleared sentries were now posted on the roofs and upper floors.[50] The remainder of 9 December was spent on mopping-up operations within the town.

10 December saw reinforcements arrive from Singapore using Labuan as an advance base. The Gurkhas were now reinforced by the arrival of the 1st Battalion The Queen's Own Highlanders (QOH), along with Royal Marines from 42 Commando these were tasked with moving further inland to secure the towns and police stations held by TNKU forces, and more importantly retake the oil fields at Seria and release the prisoners being held there.[51] After the initial setbacks a rethink was required. There was also a change of command with the arrival of Lieutenant Colonel Shackleton to take over from Lloyd Williams, while Admiral Luce gave Brigadier Glennie overall command of land, air and sea forces.[52] However, if in the event that a communist threat was established along with direct interference from Indonesia, the chain of command would change. HQ 3 Commando Brigade under Brigadier Billy Barton took over operational responsibility for the defence of Sarawak, while Glennie remained Commander British Forces, Borneo, until Major General Walter Walker, commander of 17th Gurkha Division arrived from a holiday in Nepal.[53] Walker would remain in overall command after the revolt and into the Confrontation. The next question for the land forces was how to recapture Seria with minimal loss of civilian life.

Seria

On 8 December 1962, rebel forces captured Seria police station and, in doing so gained control of the oilfields. Personnel working there were confined to their houses but were later transferred to the police station where they were incarcerated. Personnel that were deemed important to ensure the running of the oilfields were forced to remain at the oil facility. As seen earlier, Panga police station was also attacked but was able to hold off any rebel attack. Having seen or heard that the failure to secure or at least damage the airfield at Brunei Town had allowed British troops to land, this was not repeated at Anduki airfield where the rebels were astute enough to block the runway using cars, thus foiling the RAF's chances of landing troops to free Seria.[54]

British forces having failed in an earlier attempt to move inland towards Seria, were now bolstered by the Queen's Own Highlanders under Lieutenant Colonel W.G. McHardy. McHardy had been briefed by Glennie and ordered to retake Seria, but the question remained of how to do this. A plane carrying McHardy, Major I.D. Cameron, two representatives of the Brunei Shell Oil Company and Police Commissioner Mr Outram flew over Seria and Kuala Belait to better gain a picture of what they were up against. Upon landing back at Brunei airfield McHardy came up with a two plan to simultaneously attack west of Seria to relive Panga police station and retake the airfield at Anduki. McHardy had at his disposal five Twin Pioneers, one Beverly, and a Beaver used as a mobile command.[55] The doors of the aircraft were removed to allow for rapid disembarkation, which the Queen's Own Highlanders practiced on the airfield in Brunei.

10 December saw operations commence. The Beverly containing the QOH took off and headed towards Anduki, coming in low along the beach for the element of surprise, which was achieved. The Beverly landed long enough for the QOH to rapidly deploy then took off under fire from the control tower and outbuildings. The rebels, having been caught off guard by the Beverly's landing, proceeded to attack the QOH, who were moving forward to secure

The Queen's Own Highlanders training to disembark at speed from Twin Pioneers at Brunei airfield. Operated by No. 209 Squadron, Twin Pioneer CC.Mk 1s were some of first British aircraft deployed to Borneo in reaction to the Indonesian invasion. The unit remained involved in this crisis until December 1966. (Albert Grandolini collection)

The Queen's Own Highlanders' final practice before departing for Anduki/Panga. (Albert Grandolini collection)

The Queen's Own Highlanders continuing to train for their forthcoming attack on Anduki/Panga. Note the figure nearest the aircraft is armed with a sterling sub machine gun. (Albert Grandolini collection)

the buildings and the airfield. Being more battle hardened it did not take long for the QOH to secure the airfield and surrounding buildings.[56] Captain Macdonald, who was in charge of this part of the assault, now controlled the airfield and could continue to move forward and secure Seria. But first, Macdonald had to hold the Bailey Bridge over the Sungei Bera. While marching to secure this position Macdonald's squad captured a rebel Land Rover and nine prisoners along with assorted weapons and tear gas canisters. Several other attempts were made by the rebels to retake the airfield, but now the bridge was secure it was impossible for the rebels to move back into the area. By 1530hrs all Macdonald's objectives had been achieved and his forces even manged to secure the Shell Explosives Area.[57]

Ten miles away, the second part of the plan commenced. The five Twin Pioneers of 209 Squadron headed towards Panga. On the earlier reconnaissance it was discovered that a grass airfield could be used to land the QOH. So, armed with this intelligence, 60 men under Major Cameron were loaded onto the Pioneers and they proceeded towards their objective. As 209 Squadron approached the landing zone they flew into a tropical storm. The lead Pioneer, upon landing, narrowly missed a 'Major Road Ahead' sign when it taxied to a halt. Subsequently, the remaining four Pioneers came in from the south. Due to the severity of the storm the grass runway soon became a bog, but all the personnel were on the ground and 25 minutes later the Pioneers had all returned to Brunei. By 1500hrs, thirty minutes before Anduki was secured, the police station at Panga was liberated, freeing the policemen being held captive.

With Anduki and Panga now held by British forces, the reminder of the military units were tasked with moving inland and securing major roads and buildings deemed important for the relief operations being undertaking. One such building was the Telecommunications Centre. Second Lieutenant Mackenzie and his platoon was

Two camouflaged Twin Pioneers (foreground) preparing to taxi while in readiness for troop deployment. Visible in the rear is a row of aircraft including (from left to right), a Javelin interceptor, Beverly transport, Canberra bomber, another Beverly, second Javelin, and a Percival Pembroke light transport – all of the RAF. (Albert Grandolini collection)

The troops manning a roadblock quiz a traveller. Note the rubble piled onto the road in the lower left of the image. (Albert Grandolini collection)

The Queen's Royal Irish Hussars patrolling the interior in Saladin armoured cars. The official history of the Royal Tank Regiment notes that the vehicles handed over to them in-theatre by the QRIH were 'in impeccable order.' (Albert Grandolini collection)

tasked with setting up a roadblock and holding this building. The rebels in the building had other ideas. MacKenzie's platoon came under fire from the building but a sustained burst of Bren gun-fire persuaded the rebels inside to surrender and the hostages being held there were released.[58] Now that the airfield at Anduki was secure aircraft began to fly in transport: Land Rovers and trailers, along with an Assault Pioneer Platoon to bolster the Gurkhas and QOH forces.[59] While mopping-up operations continued a group was happened upon frantically waving a white flag. It transpired that they were oil workers who had been told to continue working as they controlled the local electricity supply.[60] With the outlying areas around Seria now secure, the problem of freeing the hostages held in the main police station and bazaar needed to be addressed. Intelligence reports and information provided to HQ showed the remaining hostages were being held at the police station. These reports also highlighted that the more-hardened rebels were based there and if a frontal attack was undertaken, the rebels would have no qualms in killing the hostages.[61] What was needed was a clinical strike with the minimal amount, if any, of lives lost. The task fell to McHardy to devise a plan and enact it successfully.

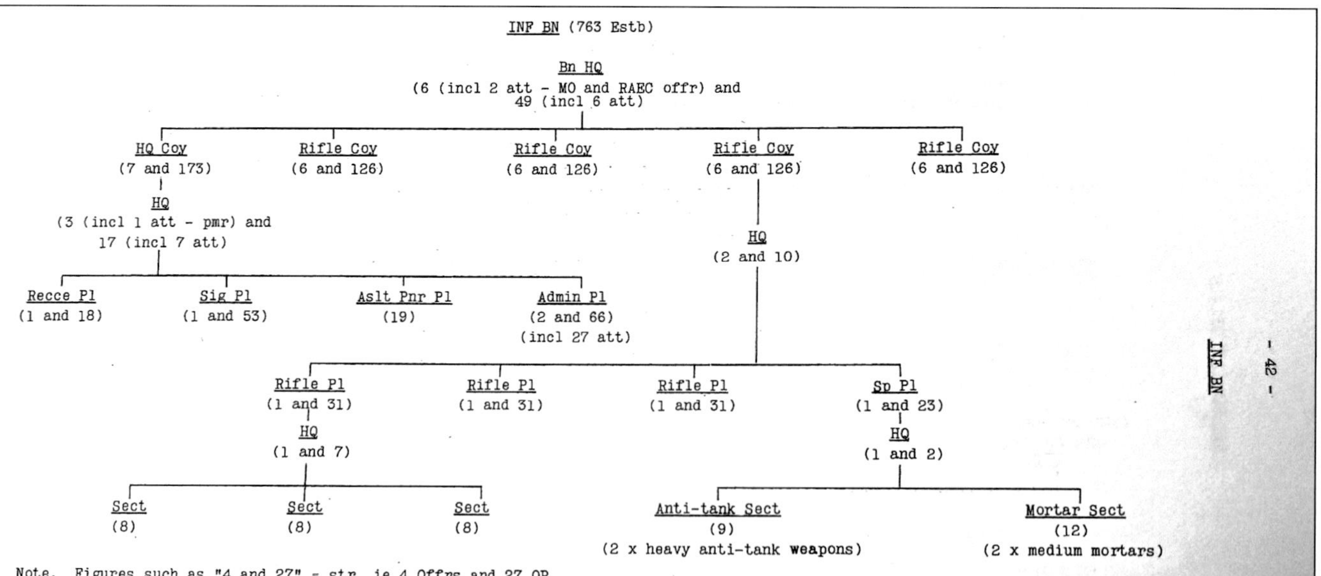

Note. Figures such as "4 and 27" = str, ie 4 Offrs and 27 OR.

SUMMARY
(incl permanently att)

Offrs	OR	¼-ton	1-ton (incl CO's Car)	3-ton	Tlrs	Heavy Anti-tank Weapons	Medium Mortars	GPMGs (SF)	GPMGs	Medium Anti-tank Weapons	Light Mortars
37 (incl 3 att)	726 (incl 40 att)	45	13	13	54	8 x 120-mm Mobat	8 x 81-mm	12 conversion kits	65	20 x Carl Gustav (84-mm recoilless gun	28 x 2-in

This chart taken from the British Army's Staff Officer Hand Book shows the 'paper' organisation of a British infantry battalion in 1963. The organisation of units was in a constant state of flux in this period as the army absorbed new equipment and not all of the heavy weapons shown here would have been of use in Borneo. Notably, this chart shows machine gun and mortar sections devolved down to individual companies as opposed to being concentrated in MMG and Mortar platoons. (Private collection)

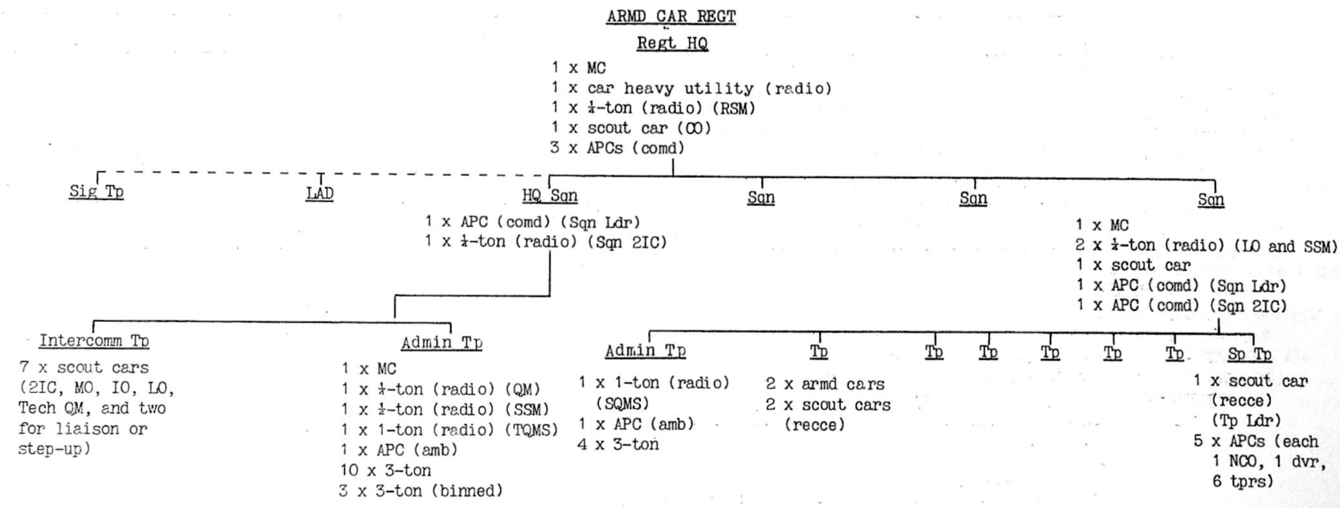

SUMMARY
(incl permanently att)

	Offrs	OR	MCs	Wheels	Tracks	Tlrs	Total Vehs excl MCs and Tlrs	Remarks
Armd car regt	42	539	5	155	–	23	155	
Armd car sqn	10	158	1	44	–	7	44	Incl 2 OR, 1 veh and 1 tlr att from sig tp and 13 OR, 2 vehs and 1 tlr att from LAD.
Sig tp	–	21	1	5	–	4	5	Incl 4 OR carried in armd car regt tpt.
LAD	1	74	1	14	–	7	14	Incl sqn sects.
TOTAL, armd car r incl sig tp and LAD	43	634	7	174	–	34	174	

This chart from the 1963 Staff Officer Hand Book shows the organisation of an Armoured Car Regiment. Troops consisted of a mix of Saladin and Ferret armoured cars (referred to here as 'armd cars' and 'scouts cars', respectively). The support troop within each squadron would often be broken up to provide dismountable support to the other troops. Individual squadrons were deployed from a number of regiments, including the Queen's Royal Irish Hussars and 4th and 5th Royal Tank Regiment. (Private collection)

McHardy firstly pulled Macdonald from guarding the Shell Explosives Area and moved him and his men into the jungle to establish choke points or ambush sites. These sites were situated along the railway line which ran south-east from Seria and east-west along an area of open land that ran through the jungle. While this part of the operation was put into action, 6 Platoon, along with the MMG Platoon and the Mortar Section, left their makeshift base advancing slowly on foot towards the police station. The Mortar Section manged to gain access to a school and a block of flats setting up Bren guns to provide covering fire if required. MMG Platoon under Lieutenant Taylor continued towards the police station. Before leaving, Taylor had been given instructions to 'get into the police station as quickly as possible with the greatest show

Saladin providing back up to a foot patrol. Note the crossed kukri insignia on the front left mudguard indicating that the vehicle was operating in support of the Gurkhas. The official history of the Royal Tank Regiment states that the rules of engagement forbade the use of the 76mm main gun. (Albert Grandolini collection)

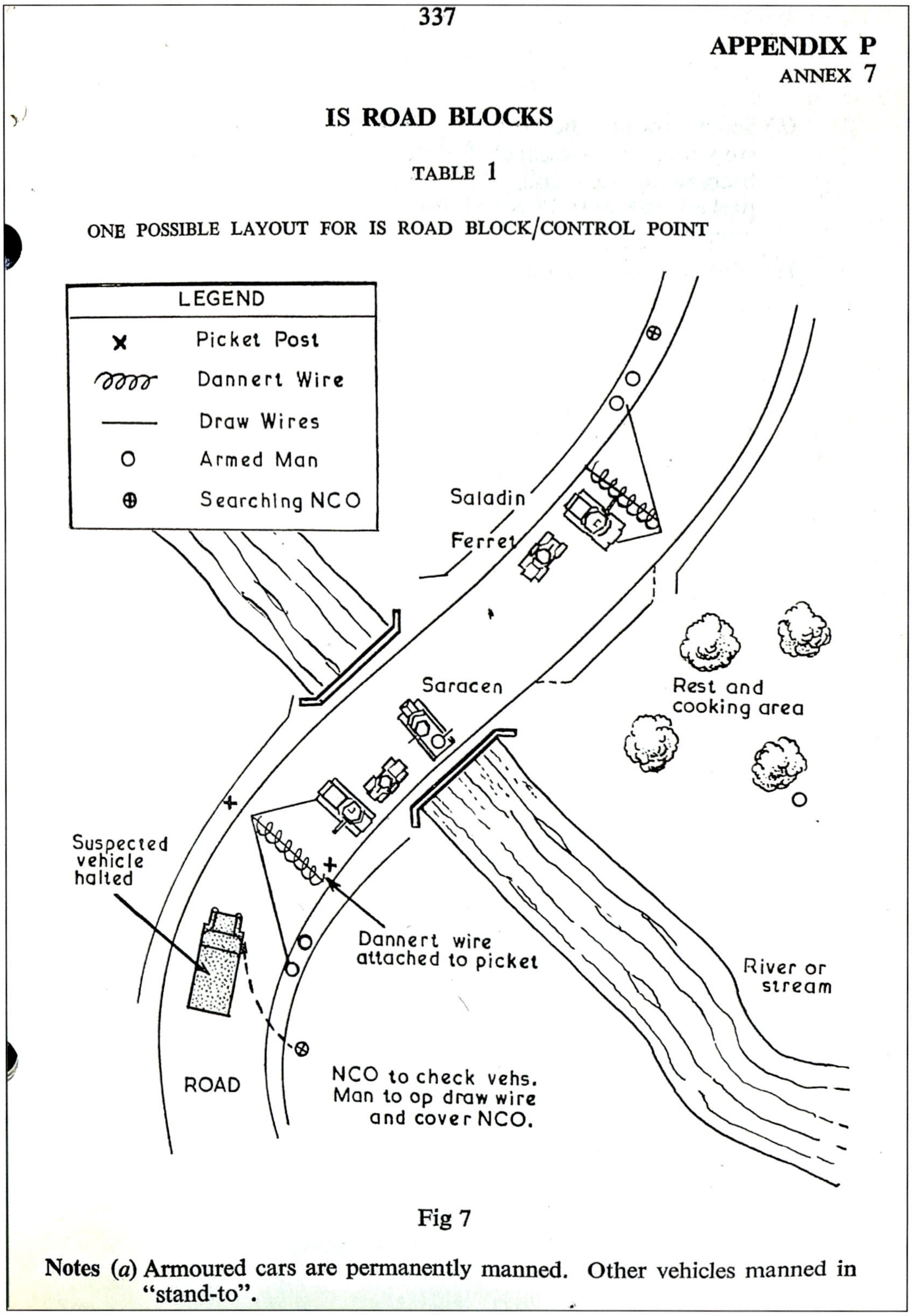

This diagram from a Royal Armoured Corps training manual issued in 1965 shows the layout of a typical IS (Internal Security) road block and shows how the different vehicles and dismounted troops would operate in mutual support. (Private collection)

of force, but with the minimum of firing.' Upon nearing the police station Taylor's Platoon came under fire from rebels hiding under the buildings and Mortar Section responded with supressing fire from the rooftops. The RAF was also involved and four Hunters flew low, buzzing the area to intimidate the rebels within the building. Under cover of the noise of the Hunters the station was rushed and, upon entering the police station, it was found that the stores and the cells were crammed full of hostages, while in another room wounded rebels were being housed. 6 Platoon cleared the building, finding no other rebels but capturing various munitions consisting of rifles, shotguns, and ammunition.[62]

Naval and RAF Support

While the land forces were continuing to liberate Brunei, with later operations moving into Sarawak, the Navy and RAF roles need to be addressed. Although the Royal Navy was not directly involved in the ground operations it did play an important role. The coastal minesweepers HMS *Fiskerton* and HMS *Chawton* patrolled the shoreline, looking for escaping rebels. *Fiskerton*'s commander appointed himself Harbour Master, Brunei, allowing him to control and operate all the available shipping that could be used for supply and transportation. *Fiskerton* was also used as a communication hub between Singapore and Brunei HQ, when the main communication line failed in the early days of the revolt. Along with *Fiskerton* and *Chawton* was the commando ship HMS *Albion*, enabling the land forces to utilise the helicopters that were onboard. These helicopters were used in a variety of roles: jungle landings, maintenance of the mobile forces operating from their bases along with airlifting casualties, prisoners, police, tracker dogs and captured arms. Helicopters were also used to fly in rice to the Iban tribes and provide parts and tools for the repair of aircraft. *Albion* was also able to supply 2,000lb of fresh bread per day.[63] The role of the Navy, therefore, was not insignificant.

From the opening hours of the revolt the RAF played an important role in the operations. During the first phase of the revolt the RAF flew 167 sorties from Singapore to Labuan or Brunei Town. They carried 3,209 passengers, 113 vehicles, 70 trailers, 13 dogs for jungle patrols, two Auster aircraft, one refueller and 624,308lb of equipment or freight. Once personnel and equipment had been landed, the RAF continued between Brunei and later Sarawak, transport flights amounted to 546 sorties, carrying 4,751 passengers and casualties, along with 1,189,160lb of freight. Total flying time amounted to 707 hours and five minutes when on active duty. Hunters flew 52 sorties during the 13-day operation to quell the revolt and a total of 837 sorties were flown by the RAF. Civilian aircraft also played a role undertaking 69 sorties. When the figures for passengers and freight are combined for RAF and civilian flights, these amount to 8,000 passengers and casualties along with 1,800,000lb of freight.[64] It was a herculean undertaking in a short space of time.

Miri and Limbang

With the towns of Seria, Tutong and Brunei Town now secure and free from rebel cells, Limbang, Bekanu, and Niah on the Sarawak side of the border now needed to be made safe. While Sarawak borders Brunei it is divided into divisions with Limbang located in the fifth division along with Bekanu and Niah. Accessibility, however, was a problem as with no runways, troops could not be flown in, the only options being by road or river. Another problem for HQ Brunei was what troops could be deployed as the QOH, Gurkhas and other services were being used in Brunei. The task thus fell to Royal Marines from 42 Commando, and 1st Battalion Royal Green Jackets. 42 Commando was given the task of liberating Limbang while the Green Jackets were initially sent to Miri and then on to Bekanu.

Limbang was situated on the Sungei Limbang and was a small non-descript town cut out of the jungle, with most, if not all, of its supplies brought in by river. When the revolt broke Limbang was quickly taken. The rebel cell of 250 men was led by Salleh Bin Sambas, a former policeman, intent on taking Limbang. Unlike when the revolt broke out elsewhere, the capture of Limbang had been meticulously planned, so all rebel participants knew their task. By 0200 on 8 December Sambas had positioned his men around the sites to be captured: the police station, gaol and the residence house. On the given signal these building were simultaneously taken. The police station presented the rebels some stiff opposition but due to fatalities and wounds received during the fire fight the station's occupants subsequently surrendered. The gaol was next to fall, allowing Sambas to free two key TNKU members Salleh Kerrudin and Haji Pilok. Kerrudin, upon his release, assumed overall command with Pilok as second in command. Sambas was told to hold the police station. Lastly the residence house was overrun with Richard Morris and his wife being taken prisoners. Initially they were held at the police station but were then moved to the gaol. Any Europeans captured were held at the hospital which was now serving as a detention centre.[65] The police station and the hospital were the lynchpin of the rebels' defensive strategy against any hostile forces. The remainder of the rebels, comprising of two companies, fanned out along the riverbank and the outskirts of the jungle. The rebels were expecting some sort of response from the British, as Yassin Affendi who was in overall command of the TNKU had passed through on his way to Temburong District having come to the realisation that the rebellion was a lost cause.[66] The rebels seemingly covered all of the key areas and in doing so had created kill boxes, the question remained as to how a rescue operation could be undertaken.

Captain Jeremy Moore MC of L Company, 42 Commando, along with 89 Marines prepared to retake Limbang. Moore's plan was to approach Limbang by river. This was a risky manoeuvre as Moore was unsure if the riverbank would be defended, but trekking through the jungle was not an option. Two Z-craft commercial landing craft were deemed sufficient for the task, but they were not armoured: if the Marines were to become embroiled in a ship to shore firefight, then the chances of heavy casualties were significant. These craft were manned by crew from HMS *Fiskerton* and *Chawton* and commenced the journey to their objective.[67] Nevertheless, the Marines had a job to do and intended to carry it out. The Z-craft made good progress and by 13 December were heading upriver, Moore perhaps still hoping that they would remain undetected. This was not the case; the noise of the boats had alerted the rebels on the shoreline and the Marines started taking fire, those on board responded with heavy machine guns.[68] They still had not reached land and were yet to secure the buildings being held by the rebels. Sergeant Smith announced to the rebels that the rebellion had failed, and the best course of action was to surrender. In response the rebels opened fire using machine guns and rifles. This resulted in two Marines killed and the coxswain in the lead craft wounded, while the second craft also took fire with company second in command and a seaman being wounded.[69]

With the Z-craft now moored the Marines disembarked and two sections of 5 Troop came ashore. Corporal Lester and his section made for the police station, while Sergeant Bickford, Troop Commander aided by Corporal Rawlinson, pressed home a frontal attack. The police station was held by Sambas who was manning a Bren gun; he was hit in the chest and arm but manged to evade capture along with some of his comrades. The remaining rebels or those who could not escape were captured. Sergeant Smith and Sergeant Macfarlane now led the reserve section ashore. Smith continued to search the outbuildings while Macfarlane moved on to the hospital. The hospital was situated near the edge of the jungle and allowed the rebels to set up ambush points. Unfortunately, Macfarlane walked into an ambush, with him and two more Marines being killed, though the remainder of the group laid down heavy suppressing fire, pushing the rebels further into the jungle. Smith, oblivious to the ambush, armed with a 7.62mm SLR and a grenade, continued clearing the hospital buildings. Hearing movement within a room, Smith prepared to throw the grenade but stopped after hearing someone singing 'they'll be wearing dark green bonnets.' Smith, upon entering the room, discovered Morris and his wife safe and unharmed. It was fortuitous that the Marines had arrived when they did: it later transpired that Morris was to be hanged on the afternoon of the 13th.[70] Once the police station and the hospital fell the heart went out of the rebellion in Limbang, although intermittent sniping fire continued for a further 24 hours. In total, Moore lost five killed and eight wounded. Moore was awarded a bar to his Military Cross. Despite these losses Limbang and the surrounding area were secure and back in British hands.[71]

While the Marines were retaking Limbang, the 1st Royal Green Jackets aboard HMS *Tiger* under the command of Lieutenant Colonel H.T. Sweeny, were steaming towards Labuan. It became clear that if the Green Jackets stayed onboard and continued to sail towards Miri it would alleviate the need to airlift them there. The only downside was that *Tiger* would have to anchor quite a way offshore as the harbour could not accommodate the cruiser. The local Resident was informed that craft were required to transfer the Green Jackets from *Tiger* to the quayside in Miri.[72]

Sweeny, upon landing, was given intelligence reports by one of his officers who had flown over their objective of Bekanu, giving a better understanding of what was ahead compared to Moore who had no reliable intelligence when he set out for Limbang. Armed with this intelligence, Sweeny and B Company, along with two sections of the Sarawak Constabulary Field Force, began the journey along the coast towards Bekanu. The plan was for one company to land away from Bekanu and march through the jungle and attack the rebels. However, the ship beached which made disembarking

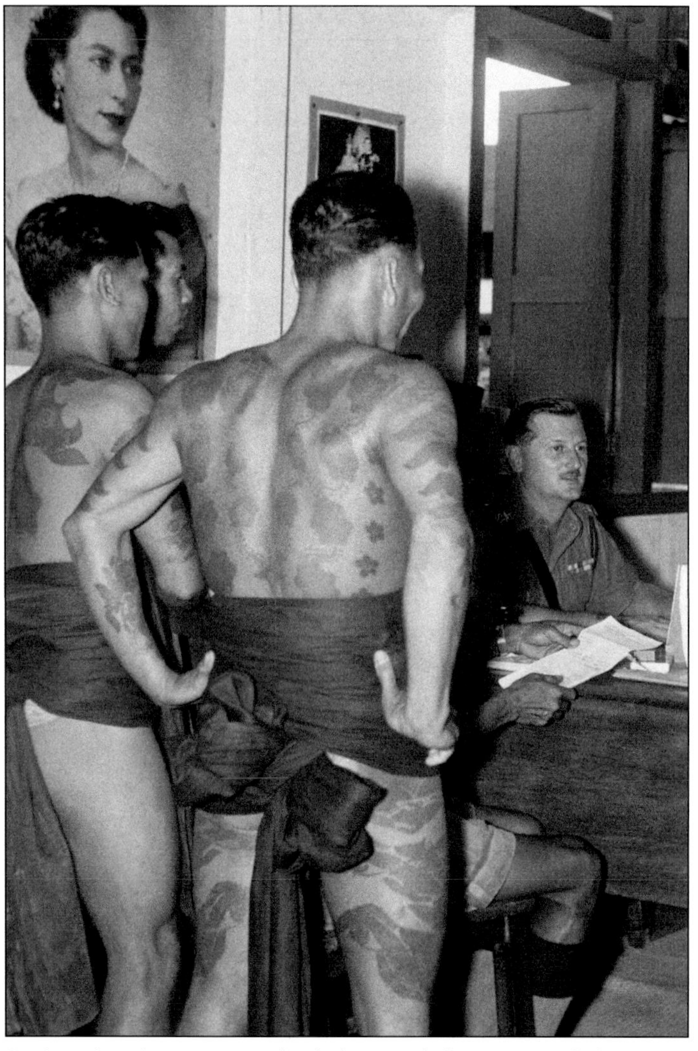

Dyak trackers being recruited to help to track down TNKU rebels in Borneo in 1962. (Albert Grandolini collection.)

and landing a problem for the Green Jackets. With one craft unable to continue, the remainder of the Green Jackets transferred to the launches which had been towed behind the beached craft and continued towards Bekanu. The march through the jungle was beset with problems with the guides making detours to avoid ambush points. Even after arriving at their destination, they still had to cross a river in boats which could only take eight men at a time. By 0930hrs the force was in sight of their objectives and ready to move when ordered. The Green Jackets had orders to retake the police station, a government building and a Chinese school. Sweeny had before the attack flown over the town and was surprised to see the rebels saluting the plane as it flew over. It was later learnt that rebel pamphlets had been distributed stating that if any planes flew over with red wing tips, they were Indonesian and friendly.[73] This was also confirmed by James Wong, Sarawak's Deputy Chief Minister, who had been held in Limbang. Wong stated that 'when the RAF flew overhead the next morning, they (the rebels) thought it was the AURI[Indonesian Air Force].'[74] When the fighting commenced the Green Jackets achieved their aims with no loss of life, with rebel forces either fleeing or captured.

Subsequent mopping-up operations were undertaken by regular forces aided by tribesmen who had been organised by Tom Harrisson who had fought in country during the war against Japan and was now the Curator of the Sarawak Museum. The men under his leadership cut off any escape routes that the rebels hoped to use.[75] Security forces remained in Brunei and Sarawak for the remainder of the year. In early 1963 a monsoon hit Brunei, so severe that Belvedere and Wessex helicopters, which had been used to hunt down TNKU stragglers, were pressed into action to rescue people from the roofs of their huts and neighbouring trees. Assault boats also came to the aid of *kampongs*, bringing food and medical supplies along with radios so that the local headmen could hear what was going on.[76] Thereby they were implementing what was to be used with great success during the Confrontation 'Hearts and Minds' campaign.

A Belvedere HC.Mk 1 coded XG476, from No. 66 Squadron, seen while approaching a clearing in the jungle, early during that squadron's deployment in Borneo. In addition to its more obvious military functions, the type was used to rescue civilians trapped by the monsoon season in January 1963. (Albert Grandolini collection)

The Aftermath

With the rebellion now broken what had been achieved? The TNKU's aim to overthrow the Sultan had failed, the leadership of both the TNKU and *Parti Rakyat* were either captured or had 'conveniently' left the country when it seemed that the rebellion was doomed to failure. Indeed, by 16 December most major towns and centres were back under government control. Along with the capture of the remaining TNKU irregulars, the authorities could say in good grace that the rebellion was over. One commentator stated that it was 'a trivial almost Gilbertian little uprising' which had been quelled with relative ease by the security forces, while Selkirk was more critical stating that 'only good fortune prevented a far more serious outcome for the British.' Selkirk continued by adding that 'the rebellion came within an inch of being completely successful.'[77] Furthermore the rebellion in Brunei highlighted just how unpopular and how little faith the population had in either the Sultan or his government which they viewed as either as incompetent, corrupt or despised.[78]

The revolt may not have achieved its aims of usurping the Sultan and overthrowing the government. But it did seriously hamper the state's advance towards representative government. While the Legislative Council was suspended until July 1963, the state was governed by an Emergency Council, despite the Sultan reaffirming his desire to move Brunei along a democratic path, which was proving very long and, winding.[79] With no new change seemingly forthcoming, by 1964, the Council voted 32 to three to establish a new 21-member council, which included 10 elected representatives, with new elections being scheduled for 1965.[80] With the demise seemingly of *Parti Rakyat*, new political parties were formed to fill the vacuum. Some were made up of former detainees while others were purported to be financed by the Sultan. These new parties were the Brunei National Organization, the Brunei Alliance and the Progressive Party.[81]

The government, in a bid to save face after the revolt, also announced plans for new development projects, raising expenditures from $16 million in 1964 to $29 million in 1965. It was also disclosed that the government, in order to maintain the peace, since the revolt had spent $5.3 million and this was the tip of the iceberg.[82] Many living in Brunei Town believed that as soon as the British withdrew another revolt would occur. Brunei was still on shaky ground and it could be argued that the Sultan, who had sat on the fence with regards to the idea of joining Malaysia, withdrew in July 1963. To this day British Forces Brunei still maintain a presence within Brunei, based at Seria, on a five-year renewable agreement with the Sultan.[83]

Djakarta and Manila's Involvement

The question remains as to whether at the time of the revolt there was any tangible evidence that either Djakarta or Manila were aiding the TNKU. In Brunei, Kuala Lumpur and Singapore the politicians, police and security forces all pondered the same question: was there any actual outside involvement? In Singapore, and endorsed by the Malaysian government, the revolt provided Lee Kuan Yew with a cover to remove those who were deemed undesirable or could hinder the amalgamation of Singapore into Malaysia. When it transpired that Azahari had met with Lim Chin Siong prior to the rebellion breaking out, Lee viewed this as heaven sent and helped him justify this arrest programme. The Malaysian government viewed the arrest programme as essential if Singapore was to join with Malaysia.[84]

In Brunei it was discussed as to whether the TNKU had outside help. This was in part due to Azahari's extensive travelling and his ties with Manila and Djakarta and that he had potentially brokered arms deals or at least procured arms for the cause. Emmanuel Pelaez, Vice President of the Philippines, strongly denied any suggestions that the rebels had approached the government with a view to obtain arms. This may have been the case, but it was widely known that Azahari had considerable dealings with the Filipinos. Even his trip before the revolt had been sponsored by the son of former president Narciso Osmen Jr, who was behind Manila's sovereignty claims on Sabah (North Borneo).[85] In the event it seems unlikely that Manila played an active role in aiding the revolt. However, Indonesian complicity is not so cut and dry.

As seen in the early chapters, Sukarno was fervently anti-Malaysian and since his victory in West Irian needed a new fight or a distraction to ensure that the Indonesian population did not look inwards and see how bad the situation was in their own country. Before the revolt occurred, the British had come to the conclusion that Indonesia was not merely keen to give help to groups within the Borneo territories ready to frustrate plans for the creation of Malaysia.[86] Once discord had been sown it could absorb these territories into Indonesia in the classic divide and conquer strategy. The Joint Intelligence Committee (JIC) had begun a report on potential Indonesian influence within Brunei, while within the Foreign Office Sir Edward Peck had already reached his own conclusions about Indonesian influence:

> The effective threat from Indonesia comes not from a possible direct attack in Singapore or the Borneo territories (in which their potential superiority in manpower and Soviet-supplied armaments would probably be seriously reduced by inept handling and planning) but from Indonesian covert support of a long, drawn out guerrilla war on the (Borneo) Border.[87]

With Sukarno now openly supporting the rebels' cause, this was followed by widespread marches within Djakarta. The revolt was portrayed at least to the Indonesians as what they had experienced in their fight against the Dutch, and as Sukarno controlled the media could announce what they liked to stoke the fires of popular support for the revolt.[88] Macmillan viewed Sukarno's rhetoric and performance as similar to those of Hitler in the 1930s. Indeed, the Commissioner General, also using Hitler as a comparison, advised the Foreign Office 'that SEATO members should realise that the Indonesians are playing with fire. We are up against a man with much of the instability and lust for power of Hitler and military forces, if not efficient, at least comparable in size for the area.'[89]

Meanwhile the Tunku, in a speech in Kuala Lumpur, accused the TNKU of trying to hand over the Borneo territories to Indonesia. The Tunku followed this up by claiming in the Malayan parliament that Indonesia had financed, armed and trained the TNKU using Malinau in Kalimantan as a base. To this Subandrio responded that Djakarta would accept the challenge.[90] The PKI openly declared their support for the revolt. In a meeting held in December, Chaerul Saleh, the third deputy premier, addressed the meeting stating that 'the Indonesian people must take immediate positive steps to assist the North Kalimantan people now fighting for independence against British colonial oppression.'[91]

This statement was further endorsed by Sukarno two days later when he announced 'Indonesians would be traitors to their principles if they did not support the North Borneo revolution.'[92] Aside from Indonesia's main Communist Party voicing its disdain at the creation of Malaysia, their support for the TNKU in Brunei allowed other communist regimes who had previously been quiet on the Malayan question to launch a major propaganda offensive. Peking and the Soviet newspaper *Pravda* provided, at least on paper, solidarity with the rebels and Indonesian complaints. Peking suggested 'that, with Sino-Indonesian assistance, the Brunei rebels will certainly be able to win the final victory.' A Canadian reporting in South East Asia wrote that Indonesia had become a front for communist ambitions.[93]

At of the core of Indonesian anti-Malayan sentiment was how the two countries were viewed and how they were governed. Sukarno's victory in West Irian allowed him to politically attack the fledgling Federation of Malaysia. Also, if the Indonesian populace was looking outwards, they would not see how their country was being governed, nor food and clothing shortages.[94] The Tunku had highlighted the differences between the two countries in a report put to the Malayan parliament. The Tunku suggested that 'in a comparison between general well-being of Indonesia and Malaysia, Indonesia showed up in a bad light.' Continuing that 'the Indonesian people since exercising their self-determination have no say in the affairs of state.'[95]

Perhaps what irritated Sukarno the most was that Malaysia was socially and economically prosperous and the Federal government represented a concept which would be anathema on some of the islands in the Indonesian Archipelago. Malaysia challenged Sukarno's regime by being a radical alternative to his authoritarian, corrupt and maladjusted centralised regime.[96] Sukarno's regime and his control over Indonesia rested on two pillars: the PKI and the army. Malaysia, or the concept of Malaysia, defeated or at least deflected the communist aspirations within South East Asia and Indonesia. These Communists wanted an ever-greater role in the Indonesian administration and also compromised the armed forces, especially its leadership who the PKI viewed as harbouring potentially unrevolutionary thoughts. Therefore, the 'Crush Malaysia' campaign was a logical consequence of the regime's unstable, authoritarian character.[97] Thereby it led Malaya and Indonesia into what would be known as the Confrontation, and which will be dealt with in Volume 2 in greater detail.

BIBLIOGRAPHY

Adams, Cindy, *Sukarno: An Autobiography* (Indianapolis: The Bobbs-Merrill Company, 1965)

Alexander, Bevin, *Korea: The Lost War* (London: Arrow Books, 1989)

Andrew, Herbert, *Who Won the Malayan Emergency?* (Singapore: Graham Brash, 1995)

Annet, Roger, *Drop Zone Borneo: Life and Times of an RAF Co-Pilot Far East 1963–65* (South Yorkshire: Pen and Sword, 2010)

Asprey, Robert B., *War in the Shadows: The Guerrilla in History* (New York: Doubleday & Company, 1975)

Barber, Noel, *The War of The Running Dogs: How Malaya Defeated the Communist Guerrillas 1848–1960* (London: Arrow, 1971)

Barr, Pat, *Taming the Jungle: The Men Who Made British Malaya* (Newton Abbot: Readers Union Limited, 1977)

Beckett, Ian, and Pimlott, John (eds), *Armed Forces & Modern Counter-Insurgency* (London: Croom Helm, 1985)

Beckett, Ian, and Pimlott, John (eds), *The Dhofar Campaign 1965–1975* (Wiltshire: RMAS)

Beckett, Ian, and Setch, Eve, *Modern Insurgencies and Counter-Insurgencies: Guerrillas and their Opponents since 1750* (London: Routledge, 2001)

Beckett, Ian, *Encyclopedia of Guerrilla Warfare* (California: ABC-Clio, 1999)

Bijl, Nick van der, *Confrontation: The War with Indonesia 1962–1966* (South Yorkshire: Pen and Sword, 2007)

Brackman, Arnold C., *Southeast Asia's Second Front: The Power Struggle in the Malay Archipelago* (London: Pall Mall Press, 1966)

Brodhurst, Robin, *The Bramall Papers: Reflections on War and Peace* (South Yorkshire: Pen and Sword, 2018)

Bullock, Christopher, *Journeys Hazardous: Gurkha Clandestine Operations: Borneo 1965* (Salisbury: Square One Publications, 2007)

Chapman, F. Spencer, *The Jungle is Neutral: A Soldier's Three-Year Jungle Escape from the Japanese Army* (London: The Reprint Society 1949)

Church, Peter, *A Short History of South-East Asia* (Singapore: John Wiley & Sons, 2003)

Clayton, Anthony, *The Wars of French Decolonization* (London: Longman, 1994)

Cross, J.P., *A Face Like a Chicken's Backside* (London: Greenhill Books, 1996)

Cross, J.P., *Jungle Warfare: Experiences & Encounters* (South Yorkshire: Pen and Sword, 2008)

Crouch, Harold, *The Army and Politics in Indonesia* (Singapore: Equinox Publishing, 2007)

Darwin, John, *Britain and Decolonisation: The Retreat from Empire in the Post-War World* (Basingstoke: Macmillan, 1988)

Dennis, Peter, and Grey, Jeffery, *Emergency and Confrontation: Australian Military Operations in Malaya and Borneo 1950–1966* (Australia: Allen and Unwin, 1996)

Dewar, Michael, *Brush Fire Wars: Minor Campaigns of the British Army since 1945* (London: Robert Hale, 1984)

Dickens, Peter, *SAS: Secret War in South-East Asia* (London: Green Hill Books, 2003)

Easter, David, *Britain and the Confrontation with Indonesia, 1960–66* (London: Tauris Academic Studies, 2004)

Flintham, Victor, *Air Wars and Aircraft: A Detailed Record of Air Combat, 1945 to the Present* (London: Arms and Armour Press, 1989)

Fowler, Will, *Britain's Secret War: The Indonesian Confrontation 1962–66* (Oxford: Osprey Publishing, 2006)

Greenberg, Lawrence M., *The Hukbalahap Insurrection: A Case Study of a Successful Anti-Insurgency Operation in the Philippines 1946–1955* (Washington DC: U.S. Army Center of Military History, 1987)

Gregorian, Raffi, *The British Army, The Gurkhas and Cold War Strategy in the Far East, 1947–1954* (Basingstoke: Palgrave, 2002)

Guleij, Ron, & Knaap, Gerrit (eds), *The Dutch East India Company Book* (Netherlands: WBooks, 2018)

Hamilton, Donald W., *The Art of Insurgency: American Military Policy and the Failure of Strategy in Southeast Asia* (Westpoint: Praeger, 1998)

Hickey, Michael, *Korean War: The West Confronts Communism 1950–1953* (London: John Murray, 2000)

Jackson, General Sir William, *Withdrawal from Empire: A Military View* (London: Batsford Ltd, 1986)

James, Harold, & Small-Sheil, Denis, *The Undeclared War: The Story of the Indonesian Confrontation 1962–66* (London: Leo Cooper, 1971)

Jones, Matthew, *Conflict and Confrontation in South East Asia 1961–1965: Britain, the United States, Indonesia and the Creation of Malaya* (Cambridge: Cambridge University Press, 2002)

Keay, John, *The Honourable Company: A History of the English East India Company* (London: Harper Collins, 1991)
Kelly, Mike, *The Last Conflict: The Durham Light Infantry Borneo 1966* (Trowbridge: Broadcast Books, 2004)
Kin, Wah Chin, *The Defence of Malaysia and Singapore, The Transformation of a Security System 1957–1971* (Cambridge: Cambridge University Press, 1983)
Kitson, Frank, *Bunch of Five* (London: Faber, 1977)
Kitson, Frank, *Low Intensity Operations: Subversion, Insurgency and Peacekeeping* (London: Faber, 1991)
Lee, Kuan Yew, *From Third World to First: Singapore and the Asian Economic Boom* (New York: Harper Collins, 2011)
Legge, J. D., *Sukarno: A Political Biography* (London: Penguin Books, 1972)
Mackie, J.A.C., *Konfrontasi: The Indonesia-Malaysia Dispute 1963–1966* (London: Oxford University Press, 1974)
Majdalany, Fred, *State of Emergency: The Full Story of the Mau Mau* (London: Longmans, 1962)
Miller, Harry, *Prince and Premier: A Biography of Tunku Abdul Rahman Putra Al-Haj, First Prime Minister of the Federation of Malaya* (London: George G. Harrap & Co, 1959)
Milne, R. S. & Ratnam, K. J., *Malaysia: New States in a New Nation Political Development of Sarawak and Sabah in Malaysia* (London: Routledge, 2016)
Mockaitis, Thomas R, *British Counterinsurgency 1919–60* (London: Macmillan, 1990)
Mockaitis, Thomas R, *British Counterinsurgency in the Post-Imperial Era* (Manchester: Manchester University Press, 1995)
Morris, Aaron, *Counterinsurgency in Paradise: Seven Decades of Civil War in the Philippines* (Solihull: Helion & Company, 2016)
Nasution, Abdul Haris, *Fundamentals of Guerrilla Warfare* (Singapore: Donald Moore Books, 1965)
Ooi, Keat Gin, *Malaysia and The Cold War Era* (Abingdon: Routledge, 2020)
Parkinson, C. Northcote, *British Intervention in Malaya* (Kuala Lumpur: University of Malaya Press, 1964)
Pocock, Tom, *Fighting General: The Public and Private Campaigns of General Sir Walter Walker* (London: Collins, 1973)
Postgate, Malcolm R., *Operation Firedog: Air Support in the Malayan Emergency 1948–1960* (London: HMSO, 1992)
Poulgrain, Greg, *The Genesis of Konfrontasi: Malaysia, Brunei and Indonesia, 1945–1965* (London: C Hurst & Co, 1998)
Pringle, Andrew, *Swift and Bold: A Portrait of The Royal Green Jackets 1966–2007* (London: TMI Group, 2007)
Pugsley, Christopher, *From Emergency to Confrontation: The New Zealand Armed Forces in Malaya and Borneo 1949-66* (Melbourne: Oxford University Press, 2003)
Rich, Paul B., and Stubbs, Richard (eds), *The Counter-Insurgent State: Guerrilla Warfare and State Building in the Twentieth Century* (Basingstoke: Macmillan, 1997)
Ricklefs, C.M., *A History of Modern Indonesia Since c. 1200* (Basingstoke: Macmillan, 1981)
Roff, William R., *The Origins of Malay Nationalism* (New Haven: Yale University Press, 1967)
Royal Air Force, *The Malayan Emergency 1948–1960* (Ministry of Defence: June 1970)
Sheldon, Walter J., *Tigers in the Rice: The story of Vietnam from Ancient Past to Uncertain Future* (London: Collier-Macmillan 1969)
Short, Anthony, *The Communist Insurrection in Malaya 1948–1960* (London: Frederick Muller, 1975)
Smith, Alan H., *Gunners in Borneo: Artillery During Indonesian Confrontation 1962–1966* (Manley, NSW: Royal Australian Artillery Historical Company, 2008)
Smith, D.E., *Counter-Insurgency Operations 1: Malaya and Borneo* (Shepperton: Ian Allan Ltd, 1985)
Stubbs, Richard, *Hearts and Minds in Guerrilla Warfare: The Malayan Emergency 1948–1960* (Oxford: Oxford University Press, 1989)
Taffinder, M.A., *Borneo Interlude: A Company, 40 Commando, Royal Marines: A Troop Commander's Journal July to October 1965* (Portsmouth: Royal Marines Historical Society, 2021)
Thompson, Sir Robert, *Make for the Hills* (London: Leo Cooper, 1989)
Throup, David, *Economic & Social Origins of Mau Mau 1945–53* (London: James Curry Ltd, 1990)
Wallace, Christopher, *The King's Royal Rifle Corps…the 60th Rifles: A Brief History: 1775–1965: From Royal Americans to the Royal Green Jackets* (Winchester: The Royal Green Jackets Museum Trust, 2005)
Watson, Barbara, and Andaya, Leonard Y., *A History of Malaysia* (Basingstoke: Palgrave, 2001)
Weichong, Ong, *Malaysia's Defeat of Armed Communism: The Second Emergency, 1968–1989* (London: Routledge, 2017)
Weinstein. B. Franklin, *Indonesia Abandons Confrontation: An Inquiry into the Functions of Indonesian Foreign Policy* (Modern Indonesia Project: Cornell University, 1969)

Journals

The King's Royal Rifle Corps Chronicle 1963
The King's Royal Rifle Corps Chronicle 1964
The King's Royal Rifle Corps Chronicle 1965
The Rifle Brigade Chronicle 1965

NOTES

Introduction

1 See Ian F. W. Beckett, *Encyclopedia of Guerrilla Warfare* (California, ABC-Clio, 1999), General Sir William Jackson, *Withdrawal from Empire* (London: Batsford, 1986), Michael Dewar, *Brush Fire Wars* (London: Robert Hale, 1984).

Chapter 1

1 https://en.wikipedia.org/wiki/Balfour_Declaration
2 Jackson, p. 51, who quoted Professor J R Seeley from 1883.
3 Dewar, p. 17.
4 Dewar, p. 18.
5 Jackson, p. 53.
6 Jackson, p. 53.
7 Dewar, p. 18.
8 Dewar, p. 18.
9 Jackson, p. 54.
10 Jackson, p. 56.
11 Jackson, p. 58.
12 Jackson, p. 58. Dewar, p. 20.
13 Dewar, p. 21.

14 Dewar, p. 22.
15 Jackson, p. 62. Dewar, p. 22.
16 Dewar, p. 22.
17 Dewar, p. 22–26.
18 John Darwin, *Britain and Decolonisation: The Retreat from Empire in the Post War World* (Basingstoke: Macmillan, 1988) p. 164.
19 Michael Hickey, *Korean War: The West Confronts Communism 1950–1953* (London: John Murray, 2000) p. 5.
20 Hickey, p. 9.
21 Bevin Alexander, *Korea: The Lost War (*London: Arrow Books, 1989) pp. 1–3.
22 https://www.army.mod.uk/news-and-events/news/2020/06/korea-70
23 See Adrian Walker, *A Barren Place* (London: Leo Cooper, 1994)
24 https://www.nam.ac.uk/explore/korean-war https://www.veterans.gc.ca/eng/remembrance/wars-and-conflicts/korean-war https://www.britishlegion.org.uk/stories/the-korean-war https://www.awm.gov.au/articles/atwar/korea https://nzhistory.govt.nz/war/korean-war
25 Fred Majdalany, *State of Emergency: The Full Story of the Mau Mau* (London: Longmans, 1962), p. 141.
26 Dewar, p. 52.
27 Dewar, p. 52.
28 Dewar, p. 53.
29 Robert B. Asprey, *War in the Shadows Volume II* (New York: Doubleday & Company, 1975), p. 965.
30 Frank Kitson, *Bunch of Five* (London: Faber, 1977), pp. 42–43.
31 Kitson, p. 36.
32 Dewar, p. 68.
33 Beckett, p. 50.
34 Dewar, p. 68.
35 Dewar, p. 74.
36 Beckett, p. 51.
37 Beckett, p. 51.
38 Many thanks to Professor Ian Beckett for providing additional information.
39 Darwin, p. 206.
40 Darwin, p. 207.
41 Darwin, p. 207.
42 Darwin, p. 207.
43 Darwin, p. 208.
44 Darwin, p. 208.
45 Darwin, p. 208.
46 Darwin, p. 209.
47 Darwin, p. 209.
48 Darwin, pp. 209–210.
49 Darwin, p. 210.
50 Darwin, p. 211.
51 Darwin, p. 211.
52 Darwin, p. 211.
53 Darwin, p. 212.
54 Darwin, p. 213.
55 Matthew Jones, *Conflict and Confrontation in South East Asia 1961–1965* (Cambridge: Cambridge University Press, 2002), p. 5.
56 Jones, p. 7.

Chapter 2

1 Arnold C. Brackman, *Southeast Asia's Second Front: The Power Struggle in the Malay Archipelago* (London: Pall Mall Press, 1966) p. 115. Beckett, p. 61.
2 See Major Lawrence M. Greenberg, *The Hukbalahap Insurrection* (Washington: Analysis Branch U.S. Army Center of Military History, 1987), Beckett, pp. 106–107.
3 See Bevin Alexander, *Korea: The Lost War* (London: Arrow Books, 1989), Michael Hickey, *Korean War: The West Confronts Communism 1950-1953* (London: John Murray 2000).
4 Beckett, p. 127.
5 See Robert B. Asprey, *War in the Shadows Volume II* (New York: Double Day, 1975), Anthony Clayton, *The Wars of French Decolonization* (London: Longman, 1994).
6 Beckett, p. 36–37.
7 Beckett, p. 132.
8 Asprey, p. 859.
9 Asprey, p. 859.
10 Asprey, p. 859.
11 Asprey, p. 859.
12 Richard Stubbs, *Hearts and Minds in Guerrilla Warfare: The Malayan Emergency 1948–1960* (Oxford: Oxford University Press, 1999), p. 55.
13 Stubbs, p. 55.
14 Stubbs, p. 57.
15 Stubbs, p. 58.
16 Anthony Short, *The Communist Insurrection in Malaya 1948-1960* (London: Frederick Muller, 1975), p. 27.
17 Short, p. 27.
18 Noel Barber, *The War of the Running Dogs Malaya 1948-1960* (London: Arrow Books, 1989), pp. 21–23.
19 Barber, p. 23.
20 Barber, p. 24. Bob Thompson, 1916–1992, became the leading British theorist on counterinsurgency. Beckett p. 235.
21 Azmi Arifin, *From Malayan Union to Malayan Emergency*, In Keat Gin Ooi, *Malaysia and The Cold War Era* (Abingdon: Routledge, 2020), p. 156.
22 Barber, p. 27.
23 Barber, p. 27.
24 Barber, p. 29.
25 Stubbs, p. 67. *The Straits Times June 17th 1948*, HTTPS://eresources.nlb.gov.sg.
26 Tom Pocock, *Fighting General: The Public and Private Campaigns of General Sir Walter Walker* (London: Collins 1973), p. 84.
27 Short, p. 72.
28 Short, p. 72.
29 Robert Thompson, *Make for the Hills* (London: Leo Cooper, 1989), p. 87. The MRLA is also known as the MNLA – the Malayan National Liberation Army – and is often considered a more exact and accurate translation from Chinese.
30 Stubbs, p. 70.
31 Stubbs, p. 70. Malcolm MacDonald, 1901–1981, was the son of Ramsey MacDonald, a former Prime Minister of Britain.
32 Stubbs, p. 70.
33 Stubbs, p. 70.
34 Pocock, p. 86.
35 Pocock, p. 86.
36 Thompson, p. 88.
37 Pocock, p. 87.
38 Pocock, p. 88.
39 Pocock, p. 88. Conversation with S Davis, Lance Corporal, retired, 2nd Battalion Royal Green Jackets.
40 Pocock, p. 88.
41 Pocock, p. 89.
42 Thompson, p. 92, Beckett, p. 27. Lieutenant General Sir Harold Rawdon Briggs 1894–1952.
43 Short, p. 234.
44 Short, p. 234.
45 Thompson, p. 93, Beckett, p. 27.
46 Beckett, p. 27, Thompson, p. 93.
47 Short, p 237.
48 Short, p. 236.
49 Short, p. 237.
50 Short, p. 238.
51 Short, p. 238.
52 Short, p. 239.
53 Short, p. 240.
54 Short, p. 240.
55 Stubbs, p. 102.
56 Stubbs, p. 103.
57 Stubbs, p. 105.
58 Malcolm R. Postgate, *Operation Firedog: Air Support in the Malayan Emergency 1948–1960* (London: HMSO, 1992), p. 9.
59 Stubbs, p. 107.
60 Stubbs, pp. 107–111.
61 Stubbs, p. 112.
62 Stubbs, p. 113.
63 Short, p. 241–242.
64 Short, p. 243.
65 Short, p. 243.
66 Short, p. 244.
67 Short, p. 244.
68 Herbert Andrew, *Who Won the Malayan Emergency?* (Singapore: Graham Brash, 1995). Andrew was a serving police officer during the Emergency.
69 Postgate, p. 5.

70 Postgate, p. 5.
71 Postgate, p. 5.
72 Postgate, p. 5.
73 Postgate, p. 6.
74 Postgate, p. 6.
75 Postgate, p. 6.
76 Victor Flintham, *Air Wars and Aircraft: A Detailed Record of Air Combat, 1945 to the Present* (London: Arms and Armour Press, 1989), pp. 335–336.
77 Postgate, p. 15.
78 Postgate, p. 15.
79 Postgate, p. 15.
80 Postgate, p. 16.
81 Postgate, p. 16.
82 Postgate, p. 16.
83 Stubbs, p. 133.
84 Stubbs, p. 133.
85 Stubbs, p. 134.
86 Short, pp. 303–304.
87 Short, p. 305.
88 Short, p. 310.
89 Short, p. 313.
90 Barber, p. 162.
91 Barber, p. 162.
92 Stubbs, p. 140, Beckett, p. 230, Field Marshall Sir Gerald Templer 1898–1979, Short, p. 326.
93 Stubbs, p. 140.
94 Short, p. 327.
95 Short, p. 330.
96 Stubbs, p. 140.
97 Stubbs, p. 142.
98 Stubbs, p. 145.
99 Stubbs, p. 145.
100 Stubbs, pp. 147–148.
101 Stubbs, p. 157.
102 Stubbs, p. 157.
103 Stubbs, p. 158.
104 Stubbs, p. 158.
105 Stubbs, p. 159.
106 Stubbs, p. 159.
107 Stubbs, p. 164.
108 Stubbs, p. 164
109 Stubbs, p. 164.
110 Stubbs, p. 165.
111 Barber, p. 188.
112 Barber, p. 188.
113 Barber, p. 188.
114 Barber, p. 189.
115 Barber, p. 190.
116 Barber, pp. 192–193.
117 Barber, p p. 209–211.
118 Barber, pp. 219–223.
119 Barber, p. 223.
120 Barber, p. 224.
121 Barber, p. 225.
122 Barber, pp. 225–227.
123 Barber, pp. 230–231.
124 Barber, p. 234.
125 Stubbs, p. 225.
126 Stubbs, p. 226.
127 Stubbs, p. 226.
128 Short, p. 463. The spelling of Maidin seems to vary, Stubbs uses Mydin (p. 226) both maybe are correct.
129 Short, p. 463.
130 Stubbs, p. 227.
131 Stubbs, p. 227.
132 Stubbs, p. 227.
133 Stubbs, pp. 240–241.
134 Ong Weichong, *Malaysia's Defeat of Armed Communism: The Second Emergency, 1968–1989* (Routledge: Abingdon, 2015).

Chapter 3

1 David Easter, *Britain and the Confrontation with Indonesia, 1960–66* (London: Tauris Academic Studies, 2004) p. 5.
2 Easter, p. 5.
3 Matthew Jones, *Conflict and Confrontation in South East Asia 1961–1965* (Cambridge: Cambridge University Press, 2002), p. 61.
4 Jones, p. 61.
5 Jones, p. 61.
6 Easter, p. 6.
7 Easter, p. 6.
8 Easter, p. 7.
9 Jones, p. 67.
10 Jones, p. 67.
11 Easter, p. 6.
12 Easter, p. 6.
13 Jones, p. 65.
14 Lee Kuan Yew, *From Third World to First* (New York: Harper Collins Business, 2011).
15 J.A.C. Mackie, *Konfrontasi: The Indonesia-Malaysia Dispute 1963–1966* (London: Oxford University Press, 1974), p. 40.
16 Mackie, p. 40.
17 Jones, p. 69.
18 Mackie, p. 40.
19 Jones, p. 69.
20 Jones, p. 66.
21 Jones, p. 66.
22 Easter, p. 6.
23 Easter, p. 6.
24 Easter, pp. 6–7.
25 Easter, p. 7.
26 Easter, p. 9.
27 Easter, p. 9.
28 Easter, p. 10.
29 Easter, p. 10.
30 Easter, p. 10.
31 Easter, p. 10.
32 Easter, p. 11.
33 Jones, p. 72. For an in-depth study of the politics within Sarawak and Sabah see also R. S Milne, & K. J. Ratnam, *Malaysia: New States in a New Nation Political Development of Sarawak and Sabah in Malaysia* (London: Routledge, 2016).
34 Jones, p. 73.
35 Mackie, p. 42.
36 Mackie, p. 44.
37 Mackie, pp. 44–45.
38 Jones, p. 75.
39 Easter, p. 25.
40 Mackie, p. 103.
41 Mackie, p. 104.
42 Mackie, p. 104.
43 Jones, p. 98.
44 Jones, pp. 100–101.
45 Jones, pp. 100–101.
46 Jones, p. 104.
47 Mackie, p. 105.
48 Mackie, p. 105.
49 Mackie, p. 105.
50 Mackie, p. 106.
51 *The Straits Times 28 September 1962*, HTTPS://eresources.nlb.gov.sg.
52 Arnold C. Brackman, *Southeast Asia's Second Front* (London: Pall Mall Press, 1966), p. 179.
53 Brackman, p. 179.
54 Brackman, p. 180.
55 Brackman, p. 181.
56 Brackman, p. 181.
57 Brackman, p. 182.
58 Brackman, p. 190.
59 Mackie, p. 160.
60 Jones, pp. 176–177.
61 Mackie, pp. 157–158.
62 Jones, p. 175.
63 Mackie, p. 160.
64 Mackie, p. 162.
65 Mackie, p. 162.
66 Easter, p. 57.
67 Easter, p. 59.
68 Easter, p. 59.

69 Easter p. 59.
70 Easter p. 60.
71 Easter p. 61.
72 Easter p. 60.
73 Easter p. 61.
74 Easter p. 61.
75 Easter p. 62.

Chapter 4

1 Cindy Adams, *Sukarno: An Autobiography* (New York: Bobbs-Merrill, 1965), J. D. Legge, *Sukarno: A Political Biography* (Harmondsworth: Penguin Books, 1972).
2 Peter Church, ed. *A Short History of South East Asia* (Singapore: John Wiley & Sons, 2003), pp. 1–7.
3 Harold James & Denis Small-Sheil, *The Undeclared War: The Story of the Indonesian Confrontation 1962–66* (London: Leo Cooper, 1971), p. 20.
4 Greg Poulgrain, *The Genesis of Konfrontasi: Malaysia, Brunei and Indonesia, 1945-1965* (London: C Hurst & Co, 1998), p. 87.
5 Poulgrain, p. 100.
6 Brackman, p. 139.
7 Brackman, p. 137.
8 James, p p. 20–21.
9 Greg Poulgrain, p. 207.
10 Poulgrain, p. 208.
11 Nick van der Bijl, *Confrontation: The War with Indonesia 1962–1966* (South Yorkshire: Pen & Sword, 2007), p. 30. E.D. Smith, *Counter-Insurgency Operations 1: Malaya and Borneo* (Shepperton: Ian Allan Ltd, 1985), p. 48.
12 Brackman, p. 138.
13 Brackman, p. 139.
14 Mackie, p. 114.
15 Brackman, p. 139.
16 Brackman, p. 139.
17 Brackman, p. 139.
18 Mackie, p. 115.
19 Mackie, p. 116.
20 Mackie, p. 116.
21 Mackie, p. 116.
22 Van der Bijl, p. 31.
23 Easter, p. 26.
24 Van der Bijl, p. 30.
25 Smith, p. 48.
26 Mackie, p. 117.
27 Mackie, p. 117.
28 Easter, p. 28.
29 Easter, p. 28.
30 Easter, p. 29.
31 Easter, p. 29.
32 James & Small-Sheil, p. 19.
33 Flintham, pp. 338–339.
34 James & Small-Sheil, p. 22.
35 James & Small-Sheil, p. 22.
36 James & Small-Sheil, p. 22.
37 James & Small-Sheil, p. 23.
38 James & Small-Sheil, p. 23. Smith, p. 50.
39 Mackie, p. 118.
40 Mackie, p. 118.
41 James & Small-Sheil, p. 23.
42 Smith, p. 48.
43 Jones, p. 111.
44 Smith, p. 50.
45 James & Small-Sheil, p. 29.
46 James & Small-Sheil, p. 25 and Smith, p. 50.
47 James & Small-Sheil, p. 26.
48 James & Small-Sheil, p. 26.
49 James & Small-Sheil, p. 26.
50 James & Small-Sheil, p. 27.
51 Jones, p. 110.
52 James & Small-Sheil, p. 28.
53 Van der Bijl, p. 32.
54 James & Small-Sheil, p. 29.
55 James & Small-Sheil, p. 30.
56 Smith, p. 50, James & Small-Sheil, p. 30.
57 James & Small-Sheil, p. 30.
58 James & Small-Sheil, p. 32.
59 James & Small-Sheil, p. 32.
60 James & Small-Sheil, p. 33.
61 James & Small-Sheil, p. 36.
62 James & Small-Sheil, pp. 36–37.
63 James & Small-Sheil, pp. 38–39.
64 James & Small-Sheil, p. 39.
65 James & Small-Sheil, p. 40. Van der Bijl, p. 32.
66 James & Small-Sheil, p. 41.
67 Van der Bijl, p. 32.
68 Smith, p. 52.
69 James & Small-Sheil, p 44.
70 James & Small-Sheil, p 45. Smith p. 52.
71 Smith, p. 52 Van der Bijl, p. 32.
72 James & Small-Sheil, p. 47.
73 James & Small-Sheil, p. 48.
74 Brackman, p. 145.
75 James & Small-Sheil, p52.
76 Van der Bijl, p. 36.
77 Jones, p. 111.
78 Jones, p. 113
79 Brackman, p. 144.
80 Brackman, p. 144.
81 Brackman, p. 144.
82 Brackman, p. 144.
83 https://en.wikipedia.org/wiki/British_Forces_Brunei.
84 Jones, p. 117.
85 Brackman, p. 145.
86 Jones, p. 116.
87 Jones, p. 116. Sir Edward Peck, 5 October 1915–24 July 2009.
88 Brackman, p. 147.
89 Jones, p. 115.
90 Jones, p. 114.
91 Brackman, p. 148.
92 Brackman, p. 148.
93 Brackman, p. 150.
94 Brackman, p. 151.
95 Brackman, p. 151
96 Brackman, p. 151.
97 Brackman, p. 156.

ABOUT THE AUTHOR

Born in 1966, Dr Adam Davis is a freelance historian and classic car restorer. Formerly of the University of Bedfordshire, he now lives in Devon. His first book, *The Furthest Garrison* covered the Imperial Regiments in New Zealand of 1840–1866. Being born in Malaysia helped cement interest in the area in particular, and his speciality is the military history of Australasia and South East Asia.